Science
for All
Children

■ ■ ■

Project Sponsors

National Science Foundation
U.S. Department of Education
Bayer Foundation
Bristol-Myers Squibb Foundation, Inc.
Digital Equipment Corporation
The Dow Chemical Company Foundation
Hewlett-Packard Company

This project was supported, in part,
by the
National Science Foundation
Opinions expressed are those of the authors
and not necessarily those of the Foundation

This material is based upon work supported by the National Science Foundation under Grant No. TPE-9153780. Any opinions, findings, and conclusions or recommendations expressed in this material are those of the authors and do not necessarily reflect the views of the National Science Foundation.

Science for All Children

■ ■ ■

A Guide to Improving Elementary Science Education in Your School District

NATIONAL SCIENCE RESOURCES CENTER

NATIONAL ACADEMY OF SCIENCES • SMITHSONIAN INSTITUTION

NATIONAL ACADEMY PRESS

Washington, D.C. 1997

National Academy Press, 2101 Constitution Avenue, N.W., Washington, DC 20418
The views expressed in this book are solely those of its contributors and do not necessarily reflect the views of the National Academy of Sciences or the Smithsonian Institution.

Library of Congress Cataloging-in-Publication Data
Science for all children: a guide to improving science education in your school district / National Science Resources Center, National Academy of Sciences [and] Smithsonian Institution.
    p.   cm.
   Includes bibliographical references and index.
   ISBN 0-309-05297-1
   1. Science—Study and teaching (Elementary)—United States.
2. Science—Study and teaching (Elementary)—United States—Case studies. 3. Problem-based learning—United States. 4. Problem-based learning—United States—Case studies. I. National Science Resources Center (U.S.)
LB1585.3.S388 1996
372.3´5´044—dc20   96-33372
                                    CIP

Printed in the United States of America

National Science Resources Center
Arts and Industries Building
Room 1201
Smithsonian Institution
Washington, DC 20560

Douglas Lapp, Executive Director
Sally Goetz Shuler, Deputy Director for Development, External Relations, and Outreach
Evelyn M. Ernst, Information Dissemination Director
Patricia K. Freitag, Science and Technology for Children Project Director
Dean Trackman, Publications Director

Science for All Children Staff
Marilyn Fenichel, Project Director
Linda Harteker, Development Editor
Cynthia Allen, Editor
Max-Karl Winkler, Cover Illustration

National Academy Press
Sally Stanfield, Editorial Coordination
Francesca Moghari, Art Director
Linda C. Humphrey, Book Design

First printing, January 1997
Second printing, September 1997
Third printing, April 1999
Fourth printing, October 2000

Contents

Part 3
Inquiry-Centered Science in Practice   133

Foreword

The *National Science Education Standards* was published recently by the National Research Council, the operating arm of the National Academy of Sciences and the National Academy of Engineering. That consensus document, four years in the making, is designed to help the country reach an important national goal—achieving scientific literacy for all students in the 21st century. As the *Standards* reminds us, "scientific literacy enables people to use scientific issues and processes in making personal decisions and to participate in discussions of scientific issues that affect society."

The National Science Education Standards present a bold vision of a new science education system. They identify what high school graduates should understand and be able to do. They describe conditions that schools must create to ensure that all students have the opportunity to learn and all teachers have the opportunity to teach. They emphasize the importance of transforming schools into educational communities where students actively engage in scientific inquiry as a way to gain knowledge and an understanding of the world. And they stress the importance of schools and school systems in which teachers are supported and empowered to make decisions that are crucial for effective learning.

In many school districts nationwide, scientists have assumed a key role in science education reform. Through partnerships with academic institutions and corporations, those scientists have assisted teachers behind the scenes and in the classroom. The Standards envision an education system that invites a greatly increased involvement of scientists and other members of the community in constantly improving the system as a whole.

As school districts undertake the challenge of implementing the recommendations in the National Science Education Standards, they can benefit by modeling their efforts on the extensive work the National Science Resources Center (NSRC) has done in reforming elementary science education in school districts across the nation. *Science for All Children: A Guide to Improving Elementary Science Education in Your School District* presents the NSRC's strategic planning model for bringing about districtwide elementary science reform.

The NSRC has made many significant contributions to science education reform since its inception in 1985. In addition to developing the Science and Technology for Children program, an inquiry-centered science curriculum for grades 1 through 6, the NSRC has been active in other areas of science reform—including disseminating information on science teaching resources, preparing school district leaders to spearhead science education reform, and providing technical assistance to school districts. These programs have had a significant impact on science education in many school districts throughout the country.

The NSRC's sponsoring organizations, the National Academy of Sciences and the Smithsonian Institution, take great pride in the publication of this book. The transformation of science education in America to enable all children to achieve scientific literacy is a challenging task, and it will require strategic thinking throughout the next decade. The well-tested plan of action contained in this book will help make this task easier, and it should be welcomed by all those interested in improving the science education of elementary school children.

Bruce M. Alberts   **I. Michael Heyman**
President   *Secretary*
National Academy of Sciences   *Smithsonian Institution*

Preface

On behalf of the National Science Resources Center (NSRC), I am pleased to introduce readers to *Science for All Children: A Guide to Improving Elementary Science Education in Your School District.* This book is a flagship publication for the NSRC. It marks the first time that the NSRC's model for science education reform has been published and disseminated widely.

The NSRC's model is based largely on experience gleaned from two primary sources. The first is the accomplishments of pioneering school districts that put effective elementary science programs in place in the 1970s and 1980s; the second is the NSRC's own work with school districts through our Elementary Science Education Leadership Institute program. Through these efforts, we have learned that it is essential to view the science program as a cohesive system that includes the following key elements: a research-based, inquiry-centered science curriculum; professional development; materials support; appropriate assessment strategies; and community and administrative support. These elements must work together to create an interdependent system. The system can be modified to meet the needs of all kinds of school districts—large and small, urban and rural. To illustrate the model's flexibility, the book includes eight case studies showing how different communities have adapted these elements to meet their specific needs.

Through the development of the Science and Technology for Children curriculum, we have also learned much about the process school districts engage in as they undertake an extensive science education reform effort. Our field-testing program has provided curriculum developers with numerous opportunities to visit school districts in the early stages of reform and to discuss with them the challenges they have encountered. This feedback enabled us to significantly improve the quality of our science modules. It also reminded us that reform is difficult and time-consuming. For this reason, school districts benefit enormously from the support of organizations like the NSRC.

We have written this book for these and other school districts committed to acting now to build an inquiry-centered science program. Experience has shown that while enthusiasm is often the initial catalyst, the school districts that are familiar with the issues surrounding reform move forward most effectively. This book presents basic information about the philosophy underlying our reform model, how to engage in a strategic planning process, and how to establish and maintain each critical element of the science program. Our hope is that school districts will find that the book helps them define an effective model for science education reform and develop a strategic plan to implement the model. The book also provides specific suggestions for overcoming challenges that may arise.

This book is not intended to be a research document or an exhaustive summary of the literature. Its primary goal is to stimulate change in the way elementary science is taught nationwide. Readers are encouraged to consult other publications, including those listed at the end of each chapter, that provide further details on particular aspects of science education reform.

We would like to thank the NSRC's parent institutions, the National Academy of Sciences and the Smithsonian Institution, for their vision and support in helping the NSRC undertake this project. We look forward to hearing from users of the book about its effectiveness, along with any suggestions they may have for its improvement.

Douglas Lapp
Executive Director
National Science Resources Center

Acknowledgments

Science for All Children has been a complex undertaking and a rewarding one. The National Science Resources Center (NSRC) would like to express its gratitude to the numerous federal agencies, private foundations, and corporations that supported this project. They include the National Science Foundation, the Smithsonian Institution, the U.S. Department of Education, the Bayer Foundation, the Bristol-Myers Squibb Foundation, Inc., the Dow Chemical Company, the Digital Equipment Corporation, and the Hewlett-Packard Company. The NSRC Advisory Board also provided guidance and direction for the project. Board members are listed at the end of the book.

Work on *Science for All Children* began in 1993, when the NSRC held a brainstorming meeting to conceptualize the publication, at that time referred to as a *Guide to Action*. Many of the participants at that meeting were asked to submit white papers, which served as building blocks for this book. The efforts of these contributors, who are listed below, are greatly appreciated.

Judi Backman
Math/Science Coordinator, Highline Public Schools, Seattle, Wash.

L. J. Benton
Program Officer, National Science Resources Center, Washington, D.C.

Joyce Dutcher
Instructional Coordinator, Fort Bend Independent School District, Sugar Land, Texas

Robert Fitch
Senior Vice President (retired), Research and Development, S.C. Johnson Wax, Racine, Wis.

Mary Kelly
Science Consultant K–6, Hinsdale School District, Hinsdale, Ill.

Michael Klentschy
Superintendent, El Centro School District, El Centro, Calif.

Richard McQueen
Specialist, Science Education, Alpha High School, Gresham, Ore.

Harold Pratt
Director, Division of K–2 Policy and Practice, Center for Science, Mathematics, and Engineering Education, National Research Council, National Academy of Sciences, Washington, D.C.

Joseph Premo
Science Consultant (retired), Minneapolis, Minn.

Lawrence Small
Science Coordinator (retired), Schaumburg School District, Schaumburg, Ill.

Susan Sprague
Director, Science and Social Studies, Mesa Public Schools, Mesa, Ariz.

Emma Walton
Program Director, Presidential Awards, National Science Foundation, Arlington, Va.

Many NSRC staff members contributed to the writing of this publication, which was developed under the direction of NSRC Executive Director Douglas Lapp and NSRC Deputy Director Charles Hardy. Special thanks go to Marilyn Fenichel, Project Director, who conceptualized, researched, and wrote the book. Linda Harteker served as development editor for the manuscript and also wrote three case studies. Her experience, humor, and support contributed greatly to the completion of the project. Barbara Johnson, Research Associate, assisted in the development of the chapter on criteria for selecting inquiry-centered science curriculum materials. Katherine Darke, Administrative Assistant, and Lynn Miller, Writer/Editor, worked on the case studies. David Stein, Editorial Assistant, compiled the materials for the appendixes. Cynthia Allen did a careful and thorough copyedit of the final manuscript and helped further refine it. Evelyn Ernst, Information Dissemination Director, and Dean Trackman, Publications Director, provided insightful feedback and support throughout the development and writing process.

The NSRC also acknowledges the efforts of 22 reviewers who critiqued a preliminary draft of the manuscript at an important stage in its development. The reviewers' thoughtful comments encouraged NSRC staff to rethink some of the ideas in the manuscript, as well as the amount of information we chose to include. We appreciate the thought and care that went into their reviews. These reviewers are listed on the next page.

Judi Backman
Math/Science Coordinator, Highline Public Schools, Seattle, Wash.

John W. Collette
Director, Scientific Affairs, E. I. du Pont de Nemours & Company, Du Pont Experimental Station, Wilmington, Del.

Joyce Dutcher
Instructional Coordinator, Fort Bend Independent School District, Sugar Land, Texas

Hubert M. Dyasi
Director, The Workshop Center, City College School of Education (The City University of New York), New York, N.Y.

George Hein
Director, Program Evaluation and Research Group, Lesley College, Cambridge, Mass.

Richard Hinman
Vice President (retired), Research and Development, Pfizer Central Research, Groton, Conn.

Kathleen Holmay
Public Information Consultant, Kathleen Holmay & Associates, Kensington, Md.

Mary Kelly
Science Consultant K–6, Hinsdale School District, Hinsdale, Ill.

Michael Klentschy
Superintendent, El Centro School District, El Centro, Calif.

Sabra Lee
Senior Research Assistant, Program Evaluation and Research Group, Lesley College, Cambridge, Mass.

Sarah A. Lindsey
Science Coordinator K–12, Midland Public Schools, Midland, Mich.

Lawrence F. Lowery
Principal Investigator, Full Option Science System, Lawrence Hall of Science, University of California, Berkeley, Calif.

Richard McQueen
Specialist, Science Education, Alpha High School, Gresham, Ore.

Carlo Parravano
Director, Merck Institute for Science Education, Rahway, N.J.

Harold Pratt
Director, Division on K–12 Policy and Practice, Center for Science, Mathematics, and Engineering Education, National Research Council, National Academy of Sciences, Washington, D.C.

Diana Rigden
Director of Teacher Education Programs, Council for Basic Education, Washington, D.C.

Lawrence Small
Science Coordinator (retired), Schaumburg School District, Schaumburg, Ill.

Susan Sprague
Director, Science and Social Studies, Mesa Public Schools, Mesa, Ariz.

Nancy Thomas
Contributions Manager, Hewlett-Packard Company, Palo Alto, Calif.

Emma Walton
Program Director, Presidential Awards, National Science Foundation, Arlington, Va.

Karen Worth
Principal Investigator, Education Development Center, Newton, Mass.

John Wright
Project Investigator, Hands-On Activity Science Program, University of Alabama, Huntsville, Ala.

Introduction

The *National Science Education Standards*, published in 1996 by the National Research Council, presents a strong case for the importance of scientific literacy for all Americans. The *Standards* emphasizes that "everyone needs to use scientific information to make choices that arise every day. Everyone needs to be able to engage intelligently in public discourse and debate about important issues of science and technology. And everyone deserves to share in the excitement and personal fulfillment that can come from understanding and learning about the natural world."

Scientific literacy is also increasingly important in the workplace. More and more jobs require that people be prepared to think critically, solve problems, and use technology effectively. Furthermore, we need a scientifically literate public if we are to compete successfully in the global marketplace.

One proven way to achieve these goals is to begin to teach science in elementary school, as early as kindergarten. Through a particular approach to science education, called *inquiry-centered science,* children learn to ask questions, experiment, develop theories, and communicate their ideas.

This book outlines a model of a science education system that fosters the teaching of inquiry-centered science. The model, which is based on research and practice, consists of five elements: a research-based, inquiry-centered curriculum; professional development; materials support; appropriate assessment strategies; and community and administrative support. These elements all work together as a unified whole, yet each element is significant in itself and must be understood on its own terms. Therefore, the book not only explores each element but also describes how they work together.

To further illustrate the ideas put forth here, the book includes a series of case studies that show how the model is being implemented in different school districts nationwide. The case studies provide evidence that by implementing the National Science Resources Center (NSRC) model for science education reform, school districts also go a long way toward implementing the recommendations in the *National Science Education Standards.*

Organization of *Science for All Children*
This book is divided into three parts. **Part 1: Building a Foundation for Change** explains the rationale for inquiry-centered science and provides some basic tools for planning for such a program. It includes the following four chapters:

Chapter 1: The Value of Science Education
Chapter 2: How Children Learn
Chapter 3: Sharing the Vision of Exemplary Elementary Science
Chapter 4: Planning for the New Elementary Science Program

Chapter 1 opens with a discussion about inquiry-centered elementary science and what the research says about its effectiveness. Chapter 2 explores how inquiry-centered science builds on what we know about how children learn. Chapter 3 presents an overview of the five elements of an effective elementary science program, and Chapter 4 discusses how school districts can begin the strategic planning process.
Part 2: The Nuts and Bolts of Change explains how to implement an inquiry-centered science program by focusing on the five elements of the NSRC model for science education reform. This section includes the following chapters:

Chapter 5: Criteria for Selecting Inquiry-Centered Science Curriculum Materials
Chapter 6: Professional Development for Inquiry-Centered Science
Chapter 7: Establishing a Science Materials Support Center
Chapter 8: Assessment Strategies for Inquiry-Centered Science
Chapter 9: Building Support for the Science Program

Science is for all students: First-graders discover the wonders of insects during a science module on organisms.

Part 3: Inquiry-Centered Science in Practice is a collection of eight case studies of efforts to implement the model of inquiry-centered science described in Part 2. The school districts and programs profiled are Montgomery County Public Schools, Montgomery County, Maryland; Spokane School District 81, Spokane, Washington; East Baton Rouge Parish Public School System, East Baton Rouge Parish, Louisiana; Cupertino Union School District, Cupertino, California; Hands-On Activity Science Program, Huntsville, Alabama; Pasadena Unified School District, Pasadena, California; City Science (San Francisco Unified School District), San Francisco, California; and the Einstein Project, Green Bay, Wisconsin.

Each of these districts came to reform in a slightly different way. Some were self-motivated and began the reform process within their own school districts; other reform efforts were spearheaded by a corporate sponsor. Still other school districts worked with members of the scientific community through a partnership with an academic institution. Finally, some school districts joined together to form consortia, another effective way to implement change.

Recommendations for further reading are included at the end of each chapter. The appendixes provide additional resources. **Appendix A** describes professional associations and government agencies involved in science education reform. **Appendix B** describes exemplary elementary science curriculum materials.

How to Use *Science for All Children*

This book may be used by many members of a school district or community, including teachers, administrators, school board members, parents, and scientists. Therefore, readers may wish to focus on the sections of greatest interest. For example, a school board president, a concerned parent, or a PTA activist may choose to read Part 1 (Chapters 1–4) carefully. It presents research data confirming the effectiveness of inquiry-centered science as well as other arguments supporting teaching in this way. This section can help you build a case to take to your school administration or community members.

Teachers and school administrators committed to inquiry-centered science will find Part 2 particularly useful. Chapters 5–9 explain how to implement an inquiry-centered science program. Important information about selecting curriculum materials, creating opportunities for professional development, setting up and maintaining a materials support center, and developing new strategies for assessing student learning is included here.

Everyone involved in education will find Part 3 helpful. The case studies explain how eight programs have implemented science education reform and explore some of the "ups and downs" that school officials and community activists have experienced along the way.

We hope that everyone who works with children and is interested in their education will find this book both useful and informative. Furthermore, we hope that it will inspire educators to become engaged in implementing inquiry-centered elementary science programs in their school districts.

Part

1

Building a Foundation for Change

The Value of Science Education

The utilization of subject-matter found in the present life-experience of the learner towards science is perhaps the best illustration that can be found of the basic principle of using existing experience as the means of carrying learners on to a wider, more refined, and better organized world.

— John Dewey, *Experience and Education*, 1938

Every fall, several million children mark the beginning of their formal education by entering kindergarten. These five-year-olds are full of enthusiasm and excitement. They will ride the school bus like the big kids and have a chance to see what school is all about. Parents, too, see this moment as a turning point. School provides an opportunity for children to discover the answers to questions they often ask, such as, How are rocks made? and Why do ships float? All those close to children hope that school will continue to spark children's natural love of learning.

Teachers use many strategies to keep that love of learning alive. To stimulate their students' natural curiosity, some teachers arrange field trips to wetlands, rivers, and lakes as part of their study of natural ecosystems. To keep young imaginations flourishing, other teachers bring duck eggs to school and encourage students to care for them and imagine what the ducklings will be like when they hatch. To instill a love of experimental inquiry, teachers use materials such as batteries and bulbs or rocks and minerals as the starting point for asking questions, experimenting, developing theories, and communicating their ideas.

All of these learning activities are part of *inquiry-centered science,* sometimes called simply *inquiry.* According to the *National Science Education Standards,* inquiry involves "making observations; posing questions; examining books and other sources of information to see what is already known; planning investigations; reviewing what is already known in light of experimental evidence; using tools to gather, analyze, and interpret data; proposing answers, explanations, and predictions; and communicating results."[1] These activities are deeply rooted in both the scientific tradition and educational theory.

Nonetheless, inquiry represents a new approach to science education to many school districts and teachers. The reason that inquiry appears new is that many districts have come to rely on textbooks as the major vehicle for conveying information to students. While textbooks may include basic information about a science subject, they typically overemphasize vocabulary and factual information. Because teachers feel pressured to make sure that students "get it all," they often ask students to memorize these words and facts. Experience has shown that memorizing words and facts not only neglects the most important parts of science but also seems boring and irrelevant to young learners.

To illustrate some of the pitfalls of the passive learning environment created by a textbook-driven science class, consider the following example, which is excerpted from a monograph written by Howard Hausman, *Choosing a Science Program for the Elementary School:*[2]

> Twenty-six third-graders are seated at tables. The teacher asks Carla to read aloud from page 56 of the textbook, which shows a picture of a farm with animals and a windmill. Carla

reads that the farm has many animals and that they need water. However, the picture shows that there is little water on the land, implying that the water will have to come from wells powered by windmills. She reads the question directly from the textbook, "What does the windmill do?"

The teacher repeats, "Can anybody guess what the windmill does? Yes, Joey." Joey, who has been skimming to the next paragraph of the text, says, "The windmill turns from the force of the air and works a pumping machine. This lifts water from the well into a water tank for the animals."

"Very good, Joey," says the teacher. "Now Carla, can you read the next paragraph?" Carla proceeds to read: "The windmill turns from the force of the air and works a pumping machine. This lifts water from the well into a water tank for the animals." She reads on about windmills operating machines to supply electric power. Then come other examples of "energy from moving air."

Several children are moving restlessly, playing with pencils and whispering. The teacher calls for attention, as he has done twice before.

"What work was being done?" the teacher asks. No answer. "Did the wind do any work?" "It blew a windmill," someone says.

The restless movements persist. There is another call for order, a period of enforced quiet. The books are collected and shelved.

The Limitations of Traditional Classrooms

Why did this lesson fail to hold the children's interest? Why were the children restless and seemingly unmotivated to explore the ideas presented during the science lesson?

For one thing, the children did not do science. They did not examine objects, observe phenomena, design experiments, collect data, or discuss their ideas. There were no opportunities for independent thinking and problem solving. Instead, they simply read about science. The children gained very little, because the book they were reading was describing things they knew or cared little about. Most children today have never seen a windmill firsthand and have no idea what a pumping machine is. The fact that a windmill can generate electricity is also meaningless to these children;

to them, electricity is something that happens when they turn on a light switch. "Work" and "energy" are abstract ideas that have never been made concrete or meaningful to them. Because these ideas are beyond the realm of their experience, the children have little desire to explore them further.

Experience is the key factor. Research on children's learning has revealed that when children do not have firsthand experiences with the things they are learning about in school, the information that the curriculum seeks to convey will often not make sense to them. Jean Piaget, a Swiss psychologist, devoted his life to observing children and drawing conclusions about their intellectual growth. His work laid the foundation for further studies of how children learn, a field that is now called *cognitive science*. One key finding that has emerged from this work is that children learn actively and they do so through direct experiences with the physical world.

Part of the pressing need for hands-on experiences stems from the fact that as today's children grow, they have increasingly little contact with the natural world. The lack of concrete experiences means that children have fewer resources to draw on in their efforts to make sense of the world. This is a drastic change from the way things were a few generations ago, when more children lived on farms and had numerous opportunities to experience firsthand many aspects of science, such as helping to plant crops and discovering the importance of rains to the harvest. Children today may see such things on television or explore these ideas by playing games on computer screens, but they seldom experience them directly. As Philip and Phylis Morrison explain:[3]

> In Abraham Lincoln's day, most of the students were from farm families. They came to school knowing firsthand about birth and death, about the full moon, about how to lever up a heavy rock, how to sharpen a blade, and how milk soured. They didn't have to learn those things in school, because they encountered them all the time. What they went to school to learn was symbols—words and forms; how to read, write, and cipher; what scholars and leaders in the past had said; how to express and reason about the world and themselves.
>
> Children still come to our schools with plenty of knowledge. They bring a wide visual acquaintance with the world

near and far, a flood of images, fact and fiction. They see print everywhere, too; signs and posters surround them; magazines and books are commonplace, with all their pictures. Television has made the wide world familiar to children. But what is deeply missing is an inner sense of the world's real constraints, of the difference between desire and performance. Pushing a button is not like leaning on a crowbar.

The symbols still need teaching; the three R's, the history, the maps, the tales remain urgent. But they lack any foundation beyond word and image. The schools have a big new task that they have not entirely realized: it is to bring in the hands-on world, the real uncertain thing that induces questioning, that stubbornly resists or wonderfully confirms what one does. What children need is to grow plants (and see them wilt for lack of water), to complete the cycle by planting the seed they themselves harvest from the plant they grew. They need to build bridges of soda straws that can hold up the weight of many milk cartons. They need to try which connections between bulb and battery produce light, and for how long.

It would be an error to blame schools for our growing lack of physical contact with the physical world, but an even bigger error not to do something about it. We are all in this bind together; it is the result of a maturing technological world where production is taken farther and farther away from the consumer. The capacity to judge from evidence when things are right, when they work or when they don't work, doesn't apply only to circuits or other matters of science. It also applies to political programs or to buying consumer goods. It is an understanding that begins with active experience in the natural and technological world.

So let us teach our children how to read, write and cipher—but let us also help them explore something of how the material world works. They need to sense through hand, eye, and mind the limits of what can be done, and how even within stern natural limits new opportunities can open.

A Glimpse at an Inquiry-Centered Classroom

Many teachers across the country today are providing the kind of inquiry-centered science experiences that the Morrisons describe.

A Problem-Solving Investigation

The students approach the problem by discussing how they could use a model of a simple circuit tester—a battery attached to a bulb with wires—as a tool to determine what's inside the mystery box. Perhaps, the students reason, they could touch the wires to the terminals on the box to see whether the device inside causes the bulb to light. Discovering whether the bulb will light will provide the students with important information about what's inside the box.

Proceeding according to their plan, the students touch the wires of the circuit tester to the terminals on the box. The bulb lights up. From this evidence, they conclude that a wire must be connected between the terminals inside the box.

As the students work, their teacher circulates throughout the classroom. She stops to talk with a pair of students. While she commends them on their work, she suggests that they take their investigation further. What kind of wire might be inside the box? Is it a copper wire or a nichrome resistance wire? Or could there be a bulb connected to the terminals inside the box? Would copper wire make the bulb shine more or less brightly? The teacher recommends that the students think about these questions, discuss possible explanations, and find a way to test their ideas through experimentation. She also suggests that the students record their conclusions, either through writing or drawing.

The students begin discussing the problem. Through the active exchange of ideas, they conclude that a copper wire would produce a brighter light than a resistance wire or a bulb. In earlier investigations, they found that both resistance wire and a bulb conducted electricity, but that neither allowed the bulb to burn as brightly as the copper wire did. Therefore, it seems likely that either a resistance wire or a bulb is in the box.

To test this theory, the students develop the following strategy: First, they will place a piece of copper wire in the circuit tester and observe the brightness of the bulb. They will hook up the circuit tester to the terminals on the mystery box. They will observe the brightness of the bulb and see whether it is brighter or dimmer than before. They will repeat this process with the resistance wire and the bulb. When the brightness of the bulb in the circuit tester matches that of the mystery box, the students will be able to determine what's inside the box.

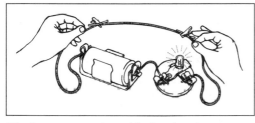

Testing copper wire with the circuit tester

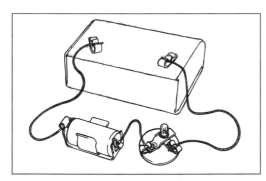

Testing the mystery box with the circuit tester

The students begin working. They notice that the bulb in the circuit tester shines more brightly than the one in the mystery box when copper wire is connected in the tester. This comparison is clear-cut, and the students easily reach the conclusion that copper wire is not inside the box. But comparing the resistance wire and the bulb proves to be more difficult. In both tests, the bulb is shining dimly, and it is hard to see any differences.

After further deliberation, the students begin to develop their conclusions. One student writes a summary indicating that the mystery box contains either a piece of resistance wire or a bulb; the student reached this conclusion because she could not tell, on the basis of the "bulb test," which of these two devices is inside the box. Another student draws a picture showing resistance wire; she feels confident that only resistance wire could create such a dimly lit bulb. When the students open the mystery box, they discover that a piece of resistance wire is inside.

The boxed example (pp. 12-13) illustrates how some fundamental concepts about electricity can be taught through an inquiry approach. The students, who are in fifth grade, have already constructed simple circuits using flashlight batteries, wires, and flashlight bulbs. They have also explored electrical conductors and insulators. In this lesson, students continue their study of electric circuits by teaming up in pairs and working with mystery boxes—plain white boxes with two terminals on top that contain an unknown electrical device. The students' challenge is to find out, through experimentation and reasoning, what electrical device, if any, is connected to the terminals inside the box.

The Benefits of Inquiry-Centered Science

For many adults, science conjures up an image of a research investigator in a white coat testing a mysterious substance in his laboratory. They see the scientific process as esoteric, with results as elusive as the potions in the researcher's test tubes. But, as the boxed example shows, science does not have to be shrouded in mystery and assumed to be too complex for most of us to master. Simply put, science is the process by which we discover how the world works, "a way of thinking, . . . the method by which the creative mind can construct order out of chaos and unity out of variety."[4] It is a process in which children have been engaged virtually since they were born, and it is mirrored effectively in inquiry-centered science programs. For that reason, it is not surprising that in the second classroom described, children were still engaged in the activity after an hour of intense work.

What conclusions about the value of inquiry can be drawn from the boxed example? The following list describes several benefits of inquiry-centered science:

1. The children are actively engaged. By working with batteries and bulbs, the children were thinking, coming up with ideas, developing their reasoning skills, and increasing their ability to solve problems. Piaget discovered the importance of using materials as a vehicle for learning and of providing a learning environment that is rich in physical experiences. "Involvement," Piaget said, "is the key to intellectual development, and for the elementary school child, this includes direct physical manipulation of ob-

A typical first-grade classroom today.

jects, the kind of manipulation so easily achieved in science lessons."[5] *Benchmarks for Science Literacy*, prepared by the American Association for the Advancement of Science (AAAS), also shares this view: "For students in the early grades, the emphasis should overwhelmingly be on gaining experience with natural and social phenomena. . . . By gaining lots of experience *doing* science, becoming more sophisticated in conducting investigations, and by explaining their findings, students will accumulate a set of concrete experiences on which they can draw to *reflect* on the process."[6] In addition, the *National Science Education Standards* establishes active learning as one of the underlying principles of science education. The *Standards* stresses that "learning science is something students do, not something that is done to them."[7]

    2. Inquiry-centered science brings the real world into the classroom and into children's lives. By bringing materials like batteries and bulbs into the classroom, we are giving children the opportunity to experience for themselves the work that scientists do. They can work with the tools of science and develop their own questions and ideas. Jos Elstgeest, a science educator from The Netherlands, defines this approach to science education by identifying it as "a swing away from the factual syllabus. Instead of teaching about scientific facts which are the result of the scientific activity of others, it becomes an education through doing science.

Instead of trying to remember descriptions of the results of science, it becomes learning how such results are obtained. Instead of hearing and forgetting, it becomes doing and understanding."[8]

3. Inquiry-centered science promotes teamwork and collaboration. Inquiry-centered science requires that students learn to work collaboratively, a skill that is increasingly needed not only in school but also in the workplace. Corporate leaders have indicated that patterns in the workplace have changed from individual problem solving to team problem solving. By working together throughout school, students have opportunities to learn from others and to discover that collaboration is essential to effective problem solving.

4. The inquiry-centered science classroom accommodates different learning styles. Howard Gardner has documented that people learn in a variety of different ways, including through language, mathematical reasoning, and visual arts. Gardner writes, "Genuine understanding is most likely to emerge, and be apparent to others, if people possess a number of ways of representing knowledge of a concept or skill and can move readily back and forth among these forms of knowing. No one person can be expected to have all modes available, but everyone ought to have available at least a few ways of representing the relevant concept or skill."[9] Inquiry-centered science encompasses many learning styles and gives children experience shifting from one mode to another. In addition, students who may not learn most effectively through traditional vehicles—such as reading or listening—have other opportunities to excel.

5. Inquiry-centered science encourages learning in more than one area of the curriculum. Science can be a springboard for exploration in other parts of the curriculum. For example, one student in our example recorded her results in writing, an effective way to develop language arts skills. The other student made drawings to describe her findings, making a link with art. Students also may be called upon to graph their findings or perform calculations to interpret their data; both of these activities show the close link between mathematics and science.

6. Children's grasp of new concepts and skills is reflected in their work during the activity. By observing her students as they worked with the mystery boxes, the teacher was able to gain important information about what they really understood about the subject. Instead of relying exclusively on tests at the end of the unit, she could assess students' progress as they worked. She could use this information to create additional lessons that related directly to concepts students found hard to understand or to ideas they were interested in learning more about.

A key objective in science education is to improve students' thinking skills, and traditional tests are often inappropriate for measuring such skills. Lauren Resnick states that multiple-choice tests "can measure the accumulation of knowledge and can be used to examine specific components of reasoning or thinking. However, they are ill suited to assessing the kinds of integrated thinking we call 'higher order.'"[10] To measure the gains made during science class, educators are beginning to recognize that alternative assessments are needed. We will explore this issue in Chapter 8.

Process Skills and Assessment

Inquiry-centered science has been shown to foster the development of certain skills needed for effective problem solving. These skills, often referred to as *process skills,* include organizing information, thinking critically, and applying knowledge to new situations. Inquiry-centered science fosters the development of process skills because it provides a firm content base from which children can draw.

Thinking skills cannot be developed in a vacuum; they evolve while people work on an interesting problem. Resnick echoes this view when she states, "Cognitive research has established the very important role of knowledge in reasoning and thinking. One cannot reason in the abstract; one must reason about something. Each school discipline provides extensive reasoning and problem-solving material by incorporating problem-solving or critical thinking training into the disciplines."[11]

Other researchers have performed longitudinal studies in attempts to measure the value of inquiry-centered science. For example, Arthur Reynolds and co-workers at Northern Illinois University found that students who had been taught science in inquiry-centered elementary school classrooms were more successful in middle school and high school science classes than were students taught in more traditional ways, such as by reading a textbook.[12] In addition, students who had experienced inquiry-centered science were more adept at problem solving than those who participated in traditional programs.

Another researcher, Ted Bredderman, summarized and analyzed the experiences of 13,000 students in 1,000 classrooms, as reported in 60 studies of science learning.[13] He found that with the use of inquiry-centered science programs, students demonstrated substantially improved performance in science process and creativity; improved performance on tests of perception, logic, language development, science content, and math; and modestly improved

Inquiry-centered science offers students time to reflect and work independently.

attitudes toward learning science. The benefits of inquiry-centered science for economically disadvantaged students were pronounced.

In addition to fostering problem-solving skills, inquiry helps instill in children a world view that reflects an understanding of the importance of science to their everyday lives. Project 2061 of the AAAS has identified five attitudes that children should acquire through science education. These attitudes are 1) curiosity (questioning, wanting to know), 2) respect for evidence (open-mindedness, willingness to consider conflicting evidence), 3) critical reflection (weighing observations and evaluating what has been observed), 4) flexibility (willingness to reserve judgment and reconsider ideas), and 5) sensitivity to living things (respect for life and environmental awareness).

Science educators hypothesize that students who experience inquiry throughout school will become questioning adults, interested in hearing all sides of an argument before passing judgment. They will be keen observers, adept at evaluating what they have seen and drawing conclusions about it. Also, they will be more concerned about the natural world and more committed to protecting the environment than previous generations have been.

Although this hypothesis has not yet been tested on a large scale, there is evidence that inquiry will result in these outcomes for one key reason: It supports the way children naturally learn. Chapter 2 explores further the relationship between inquiry and the way children learn by focusing on the work of cognitive scientists. Their research underscores the value of inquiry in fostering intellectual development.

Key Points

▶ The inquiry-centered approach to science encompasses working with materials, asking questions, planning experiments, interpreting data, synthesizing results, and communicating those results.

▶ Inquiry supports the way children naturally learn, a very strong argument for using this approach to teach elementary school science.

▶ Inquiry-centered science is easily integrated with other areas of the curriculum, such as language arts and mathematics.

▶ Inquiry accommodates different learning styles, giving students who may not learn most effectively through reading or listening other opportunities to succeed.

For Further Reading

American Association for the Advancement of Science. 1989. *Science for All Americans.* New York: Oxford University Press.

American Association for the Advancement of Science. 1993. *Benchmarks for Science Literacy.* New York: Oxford University Press.

Dewey, J. 1938. *Experience and Education.* New York: Collier Books.

Dow, P. B. 1991. *Schoolhouse Politics: Lessons from the Sputnik Era.* Cambridge, Mass.: Harvard University Press.

Gardner, H. 1993. *Multiple Intelligences: The Theory in Practice.* New York: Basic-Books.

Harlan, W. 1985. *Teaching and Learning Primary Science.* New York: Teachers College Press.

Mechling, K. R., and D. L. Oliver. 1983. *Handbook IV: What Research Says About Elementary Science.* Washington, D.C.: National Science Teachers Association.

National Research Council. 1996. *National Science Education Standards.* Washington, D.C.: National Academy Press.

How Children Learn

But there is a strong hunch that the early learning, or lack of it, is crucial; and where the early learning has been missed there is an equally strong hunch that what was missed early cannot be faked or by-passed.

— David Hawkins, *Daedalus*, 1983

For more than 50 years, cognitive scientists have been observing how children approach and solve problems. Their work has resulted in an impressive body of research about the learning process. Building on and modifying the foundation laid by Jean Piaget in the 1920s through the 1960s,[1] cognitive scientists have been able to draw some general conclusions about what is needed for effective learning to take place.

Cognitive science is a complex field. It is not our intention to explore all aspects of the field or to give a complete history of it. Our goal is to show how the findings of cognitive scientists support inquiry-centered science education at the elementary level. We will focus on two principles that have grown out of cognitive science and have important implications for effective science teaching and learning.

1. As part of the learning process, children develop theories about the world and how it works. We now know that children construct understanding and develop theories about the world on the basis of their experience. Lauren Resnick describes the process as follows: "Learners try to link new information to what they already know in order to interpret the new material in terms of established schemata."[2] The implication of this for educators is that it is important to begin building children's experiential base in the primary grades by providing research-based, inquiry-centered experiences.

2. The development of the human brain follows a predictable path. The developing biological structures in the brain determine the complexity of thinking possible at a given age. Educators must be aware of stages of growth and be prepared to teach what is developmentally appropriate for children in each grade throughout elementary school.

Incorporating these two basic concepts of cognitive science into an elementary science program can lead to the development of more effective learning experiences. In the following sections, we will explore some of the implications of these concepts.

The Role of Inquiry-Centered Experiences in Elementary Science

Educators have long debated the relationship between hands-on learning and book learning in the classroom. In the 1960s, some disciples of cognitive psychologist Jean Piaget were advocates of pure "discovery" learning; taken to the extreme, an advocate of this school of thought might suggest that the most effective way for children to learn about buoyancy would be to give them a basin of water and a variety of floating and sinking objects and have them learn what they can from these materials. Left to their own devices, some children may discover that some of the objects float while others sink. The teacher would then be requested to help the children make sense of their findings.

Because experience has shown that most children need some guidance in order to learn, by the 1970s, many educators believed that a more realistic way to organize the classroom is through a combination of instruction and hands-on experiences.[3] These educators acknowledged that hands-on experiences generate excitement and enthusiasm for children and provide them with valuable learning experiences. At the same time, the educators had come to see that it is impossible to learn everything this way; some things, such as the names of the planets and their position in the solar system or the concept of life cycles, need to be introduced by the teacher. The challenge for teachers becomes deciding how to integrate didactic instruction and inquiry-centered experiences.

In the past, many teachers have tended to rely on books and pictures to teach science concepts. When possible, some have used hands-on experiences to reinforce that learning. The problem with this approach is that students may have no real-life experiences that relate to this information. Children learn best when they can link new information to something they already know. Therefore, it is often most effective to introduce a new concept by providing children with inquiry-centered experiences. By doing so, educators provide students with a firmer foundation on which to attach the information they will receive later on from other sources. Lawrence Lowery summarizes these ideas: "Books are important. We can learn from them. But books can only do this if our experiential foundation is well prepared. To learn geometry, we must have experience handling geometric forms and comparing them for similarities and differences. To learn about electricity, we must explore relationships among batteries, wires, and bulbs."[4]

Furthermore, inquiry-centered experiences generate one of the most essential ingredients of learning—curiosity. Jane Healy writes, "As well-intentioned parents and teachers, we all sometimes end up taking charge of learning by trying to 'stuff' [the child] rather than arranging things so that the youngster's curiosity impels the process. Children need stimulation and intellectual challenges, but they must be actively involved in their learning, not responding passively."[5]

Lowery believes that curiosity serves an even larger function. He describes it as a "trigger" that helps build crucial connections in the brain. These connections enable children to synthesize specific pieces of information, such as observations of color, form, and texture of an object, into the larger concept of one object with all these attributes. According to Lowery, the ability to synthesize is the essence of intelligence, and intelligence is the product of the quality and quantity of connections in the brain. He believes that educators would do well to capitalize on curiosity in the classroom because it sparks the formation of these connections.

The Implications of Cognitive Research

Children have a strong, innate desire to make sense of the world—and for good reason. With an array of sensory information flooding into the brain, coupled with growing motor skills and cognitive abilities, it is imperative for even the very young child to organize the data.

The way children begin to structure information in their minds depends on a variety of factors, including their individual experiences, their temperament and personality, and their culture. As these factors come together, children develop unique and enduring theories about the world and how it works. For example, a preschooler may observe that many living things, such as people, dogs, cats, and birds, have the ability to move on their own. On this basis, he or she may assume that one characteristic of living things is the ability to move on their own. This notion, while partially correct, discounts plants—a whole other world of living things. Yet to young children, this theory is satisfying, because it organizes a portion of their experience in a way that makes some sense.

Researchers have explained this "theory-making" ability in children in different ways. Howard Gardner has called such ideas part of the "unschooled mind."[6] Resnick uses the term "naive theories" and maintains that children use such theories to explain real-world events before they have had any formal instruction.[7] Gardner and Resnick agree that even after starting school, children continue to hold on tightly to their early ideas and theories.

For example, consider Deb O'Brien's fourth-grade class in Massachusetts.[8] In developing a unit on heat for her class, O'Brien began by asking students for their ideas about heat. To her surprise, she discovered that after nine long winters during which they had been told repeatedly to put on their sweaters when they got cold, the students were convinced that the sweaters themselves produced heat. This was their "naive theory." O'Brien decided to give the students a chance to find out for themselves whether sweaters actually generate heat. She challenged her students to design an experiment to demonstrate "sweater heat." The students put thermometers in their sweaters to measure their temperature. Their hypothesis was that the temperature would rise, indicating that the sweaters were indeed "warm."

O'Brien assumed that after observing a stable sweater temperature, the students would realize their misunderstanding, and the class would move on. But she was mistaken. Although the temperature of the sweaters stayed consistently at 68 degrees Fahrenheit, the students did not accept this evidence immediately. One student, Katie, wrote in her journal: "Hot and cold are sometimes strange. Maybe [the thermometer] didn't work because it was used to room temperature."

The students held to their beliefs through several trials. It was only after they had done everything they could think of—from keeping the thermometers in the sweaters for long periods of time, to moving the sweaters to another location, to wrapping the sweaters in sleeping bags—that some children were willing to consider other ideas about heat. In fact, Katie was one of the first to recognize that heat does not come from her sweater but from the sun and her own body.

This example is important because it illustrates how tightly children hold on to their theories and how difficult it is for them to relinquish them, even in the face of conflicting evidence. Nonetheless, O'Brien was able to help some children replace one set of ideas with more accurate information. She did so by following a clearly defined process. First, she allowed time for the children to express their naive theories by discussing what they thought about heat at the beginning of the unit. Second, she used that information to design the major part of the unit—having the students devise experiments to test their theories. Third, she let the students use their own firsthand experiences as a starting point for reconsidering their old ideas and constructing new knowledge. Fourth, over the long term, she encouraged the students to apply that information to new situations. For example, next winter, when the children put on their sweaters, they will know that the heat they feel comes not from the sweaters but from their own bodies.

Many educators and cognitive scientists believe that this four-step process is at the heart of learning. The process is based on a theory of learning called *constructivism*. Constructivism promotes an important goal of science education—in-depth understanding of a subject, often called *conceptual understanding*. As Susan Sprague explains, "The constructivist model of learning contends that each student must build his or her understanding. In such a process, understanding can never be completed. Each student must work through his or her path toward deeper and deeper understanding and skills."[9]

The process used by O'Brien has been refined and developed into a *learning cycle* that can be incorporated into the science curriculum. The learning cycle typically includes four phases.

1. Focus: Students describe and clarify their ideas about a topic. This is often done through a class discussion, where students share what they know about the topic and what they would like to learn more about. For the teacher, this is a good time to develop an understanding of students' current knowledge and possible misconceptions and to consider how to incorporate this information into the planned lessons. This is also a time to spark excitement and curiosity and to encourage children to consider pursuing their own questions.

2. Explore: Students engage in hands-on, in-depth explorations of science phenomena. During this phase, it is important for students to have adequate time to complete their work and to perform repeated trials if necessary. Students often work in small groups during this phase. They also have the opportunity to discuss ideas with their classmates, which is a valuable part of the learning process.

3. Reflect: Students organize their data, share their ideas, and analyze and defend their results. During this phase, students are asked to communicate their ideas, which often helps them consolidate their learning. For teachers, this is a time to guide students as they work to synthesize their thinking and interpret their results.

4. Apply: Students are offered opportunities to use what they have learned in new contexts and in real-life situations.

As teachers begin implementing the learning cycle in their

In phase 2 of the learning cycle, students engage in hands-on, in-depth explorations. Here, second-graders work together to investigate soil.

classrooms, they may notice that their students seem uncomfortable or reluctant to acknowledge that their naive theories were wrong. These reactions are the result of the internal conflict many students feel as they struggle to give up one set of theories for another. For many students, confronting their previous misconceptions and modifying them represents a difficult intellectual challenge.[10] Therefore, it is important that teachers be aware of their students' struggle and be tolerant of this process and the frustration it may produce.

Ensuring That the Curriculum Is Developmentally Appropriate

While the learning cycle provides a framework for a pedagogical approach, educators must still decide what content to include in the science program. To do so, they must understand children's intellectual development. Piaget's work with children resulted in a theory about intellectual growth that is based on the premise that all children pass through the same stages, in approximately the same order, as they develop. Although many researchers have questioned some of Piaget's ideas and postulated that he underestimated children's cognitive abilities, his theories still provide basic guidelines for educators about the kind of information children can understand as they move through elementary school.

The essence of the model described below, developed by Lowery and based on Piaget's work, is that we can maximize learning by presenting science concepts to children in a way that will be meaningful at each developmental level or stage.[11] The model is based on the human need to organize the information received from the senses in logical, coherent systems. For young children, these systems may be as simple as sorting objects by color or shape. The ability to sort and recognize patterns is particularly important, because children must master these skills before they can learn to read.

Children learn at different rates, however, and not all children achieve these milestones at the same time. In general, every class in a typical elementary school spans at least a full grade of cognitive developmental levels. The basic stages of cognitive growth, however, may be summarized as follows:

▶   Through the primary grades, children typically group objects on the basis of one attribute, such as color. When discussing plants, primary school students will be able to sort them by color or size, but they probably cannot perform both steps *at the same time.* In fact, it is a major cognitive leap when children, at about fourth grade, are able to organize objects and ideas on the basis of more than one characteristic at the same time. The significance of this information for educators is that young children are best at learning singular and linear ideas and cannot be expected to deal with more than one variable of a scientific investigation at a time. For example, when observing weather, primary school students can study variables such as temperature, wind, and precipitation separately; it is not appropriate to expect them to understand the relationships among these variables. By the upper elementary grades, however, students will be able to consider such phenomena as how wind influences the perceived temperature (the "wind-chill" factor).

▶ Toward the end of elementary school, students start to make inferences. To some researchers, this marks the beginning of deductive reasoning. At this stage, students also realize that different plants or different animals can be classified into subordinate categories. For example, they understand that all crocodiles are reptiles but not all reptiles are crocodiles. At this stage of development, students are ready to design controlled experiments and to discover relationships among variables. When investigating the frequency of pendulum swings (number of swings in a minute) during a module on time, for example, sixth-grade students can experiment by changing variables, such as the length of the string or the mass of the pendulum bob, and then determining whether one or both of these variables affect the frequency of the pendulum swings.

▶ From this point on, students' thinking processes continue to become more and more complex. At the onset of adolescence, students not only can classify objects by multiple attributes, they can also experiment with different organizational strategies. For example, they can decide how they want to organize a collection of plants. They may choose to organize by color, size, shape, height, or leaf shape. They become more adept at manipulating these characteristics, which means that their scientific experiments can become increasingly more sophisticated. By age 16, students can understand highly complex organizational schemes, such as the periodic chart of elements and the structure of DNA.

If these developmental steps are not reflected in science instructional materials, there will be a mismatch between what children are capable of doing and what they are being asked to do. For example, it is inappropriate to expect a nine-year-old to understand the abstract concept of acceleration, yet some fourth-grade science programs include this concept. When this kind of mismatch happens over and over again, children do not learn as much as they could about science. Equally important, they do not enjoy science. For some children, this leads to feelings of failure and the development of negative attitudes toward science. If we can modify the curriculum to accommodate different stages of cognitive growth, we will take a big step toward solving such problems.

Key Points

▶ Inquiry-centered science provides an experiential base that children can relate to information they are acquiring through other sources. Because an experiential base is crucial for learning, it is appropriate to place hands-on learning first, before other kinds of learning take place.

▶ Children begin forming theories about the world long before they have accurate factual information, and they hold on tightly to these early ideas and theories. For this reason, educators need to be aware that it can take children a long time and many different encounters with a new concept to achieve conceptual understanding.

▶ To facilitate conceptual understanding on the part of students, the teacher needs to assume a new role in the classroom. He or she needs to create meaningful learning experiences that enable children to construct their understanding and deepen their knowledge of a subject.

▶ The way to maximize learning at each stage of growth is to present science concepts that are appropriate to the child's developmental level.

▶ The learning cycle—Focus, Explore, Reflect, Apply—has been applied in thousands of science classrooms. It is an effective way to implement the findings of cognitive scientists.

For Further Reading

Brooks, J. G., and M. G. Brooks. 1993. *In Search of Understanding: The Case for Constructivist Classrooms*. Alexandria, Va.: Association for Supervision and Curriculum Development.

Bybee, R. W., and J. D. McInerney, eds. 1995. *Redesigning the Science Curriculum*. Colorado Springs: BSCS.

Carey, S. 1985. *Conceptual Change in Childhood*. Cambridge, Mass.: MIT Press.

Champagne, A. B., and L. E. Hornig. 1987. "Practical Applications of Theories About Learning." In *This Year in School Science 1987: The Report of the National Forum for School Science*, A. B. Champagne and L. E. Hornig, eds. Washington, D.C.: American Association for the Advancement of Science.

Duckworth, E. 1987. *"The Having of Wonderful Ideas" and Other Essays on Teaching and Learning.* New York: Teachers College Press.

Gardner, H. 1991. *The Unschooled Mind.* New York: BasicBooks.

Hawkins, D. 1983. "Nature Closely Observed." *Daedalus, Journal of the American Academy of Arts and Sciences* Spring: 65-89.

Healy, J. M. 1990. *Endangered Minds: Why Our Children Don't Think.* New York: Simon & Schuster.

Langford, P. 1989. *Children's Thinking and Learning in the Elementary School.* Lancaster, Penn.: Technomic Publishing Company.

McGilly, K., ed. 1994. *Classroom Lessons: Integrating Cognitive Theory and Classroom Practice.* Cambridge, Mass.: MIT Press.

National Research Council. 1996. *National Science Education Standards.* Washington, D.C.: National Academy Press.

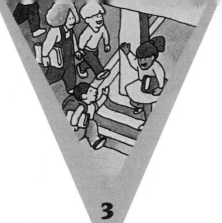

3

Sharing the
Vision of Exemplary
Elementary Science

*The more we help children to have their wonderful
ideas and to feel good about themselves for having
them, the more likely it is that they will some day happen upon wonderful ideas that no else has happened
upon before.*

—Eleanor Duckworth, *"The Having of Wonderful Ideas"*
and Other Essays on Teaching and Learning, 1987

Imagine a science classroom that
is very different from the one that most adults experienced as children. The teacher is using the learning cycle to organize the science lesson. As a result, students are up and about, consulting with
their classmates about their thoughts and ideas. In addition to
reading books, students are mixing different kinds of soils to discover their properties, observing the weather, and measuring the
height of plants growing in the classroom. All children, from the
academically gifted to those with learning disabilities, have a conviction that they can succeed in science class.

The role of the teacher in such a classroom is very different from what most people have come to expect. No longer the source of all knowledge, the teacher is a guide who listens to what the children say, asks appropriate questions, and designs activities to help these already curious children become interested in learning more. As the *National Science Education Standards* explains, "Teachers of science constantly make decisions, such as when to change the direction of a discussion, how to engage a particular student, when to let a student pursue a particular interest, and how to use an opportunity to model scientific skills and attitudes."[1]

In classrooms similar to this one, students and teachers work together to create learning communities. Creating one school, or even one classroom, that reflects this vision is daunting; creating thousands of such classrooms in districts of varying sizes and resources nationwide is even more challenging. School districts may wonder where to begin. They are aware of their overall goal; however, they cannot define the steps or processes they need to engage in to reach it.

Fortunately, there is a growing consensus among educators about the elements that are needed to create an inquiry-centered elementary science program. Five essential elements have been identified and can be used to construct a model that provides school districts with a concrete, systematic, and clear-cut path to follow.

The Elements in the Strategic Planning Model

Inquiry-Centered Science Curriculum

Curriculum materials are the "meat" of the science program—what is actually being taught to children. Although many different kinds of curriculum materials can be used to implement inquiry-centered science programs, one of the most effective approaches is to build the science curriculum around a series of science *modules,* or units, each of which focuses on a different area of science and technology. A science kit, specifically designed for each unit, includes all the materials needed for a class of students to investigate a particular science topic for six to eight weeks. Each kit comes with a comprehensive teacher's guide, divided into 12 to 16 *lessons,* that describes the activities to be completed within the module. Student activity books, with instructions for conducting investigations and developmentally appropriate reading selections, are part of the kit as well.

Professional Development

Professional development is the process by which school districts prepare teachers to introduce the curriculum materials in their classrooms. School districts can use many strategies to enhance

Early Efforts to Identify the Essential Elements of an Effective Elementary Science Program

The current science education reform movement is built on a foundation laid in the 1960s. At that time, the post-Sputnik national science curriculum reform movement produced elementary science curriculum materials that emphasized student inquiry. A few school districts started using these materials as the basis for inquiry-centered elementary science programs. These districts included Mesa, Arizona; Seattle, Washington; Schaumburg, Illinois; Fairfax County, Virginia; Multnomah, Oregon; Minneapolis, Minnesota; and Anchorage, Alaska. Today, these districts serve as a model for those just starting out.

Each of these districts initially worked alone and did not communicate with other districts. When they began to share their experiences, they were surprised to discover how similar their programs were. Each found that in order to succeed, the district needed to incorporate the elements described in this chapter into its science education reform plan. What determined the differences were local politics in the school districts and the resources available to them.

For Charles Hardy, former assistant superintendent of curriculum and instruction in Highline, a suburb of Seattle, Washington, and chief architect of its inquiry-centered elementary science program, the starting point was teachers. A former high school chemistry and physics teachers' professional development. For example, as a way of introducing the new science program, districts can hold workshops where teachers become familiar with the science content of the module and discuss how to manage materials such as chemicals, water, soil, and living organisms in the classroom. Over time, districts can follow these introductory workshops with advanced sessions, during which teachers can perfect new pedagogical strategies, such as asking good questions, encouraging students to

teacher, he came from a tradition of close interaction with his peers, so he decided to try the same strategy at the elementary level. Every opportunity he had, Hardy would go into classrooms to observe what the children enjoyed doing and how the teachers interacted with the children. Using these insights, he then worked with local teachers and curriculum developers to create an inquiry-centered curriculum for the district. Soon after, a materials center, which supplied teachers with the science materials and supplies needed to teach the curriculum, was established.

"Teacher in-service education was—and continues to be—a strong element in our program," Judi Backman, Highline's science coordinator for more than 20 years, recalls. "We know that the only way for the program to work is if teachers are familiar with the curriculum materials and comfortable teaching them."

Highline's science program began with professional development efforts and quickly expanded to include inquiry-centered science kits and materials support. Now, because of increased national interest in inquiry-centered science, Highline is developing new assessment strategies.

"We received a grant from the National Science Foundation to develop assessment techniques more in line with inquiry-centered teaching," says Backman. "When we started, we knew that paper-and-pencil tests were not adequate, but they were all that was available. Now we have some more options, so we are able to round out this element of our program."

initiate their own learning, and integrating science with other parts of the curriculum. The more proficient teachers become in these areas, the more effectively the science curriculum will be taught and the more children will learn.

Other strategies for districts to consider include recommending that teachers attend programs sponsored by professional societies such as Sigma Xi or the American Chemical Society and providing time for teachers to observe more experienced teachers, attend talks given by other teachers, or work closely with a more experienced colleague.

Science Materials Support
A materials support system is needed to ensure that teachers have access to the science kits and everything else they need to present a module in the classroom. By setting up cost-effective systems for supplying materials and equipment, school districts can remove from teachers the responsibility of inventorying and ordering the materials needed for the science lesson and place it in the hands of support staff who are trained to carry out these tasks. Implementation involves coordinating myriad details. It is crucial to plan the materials support component carefully, because a well-functioning system is essential for a successful science program.

Assessment
A system is needed to provide appropriate tools for teachers to use to assess student learning. Assessments can include both traditional paper-and-pencil tests and observations of student performance. The intent is to assess what students truly know and can do as a result of their experiences with the materials. Assessments also serve to guide instruction for teachers so that they can develop more effective teaching strategies. These new approaches to assessment are a departure from traditional testing, and teaching teachers how to use them must be one goal of the professional development program.

Administrative and Community Support
Building support within the school system and the community is critical to the success of the program. Essential elements of admin-

istrative support include the endorsement of the superintendent and assistant superintendent of curriculum and instruction, as well as the involvement of the director of the elementary science curriculum and all elementary school principals. Without their support, it will be nearly impossible to address the other four elements.

In addition, the program will be stronger if it has broad community support. Keeping parents informed about the new science program is an important part of building community support. Many school districts strengthen community support by creating partnerships with local colleges and universities, business and industry, or both. A local corporation may agree to allocate space that can be used to house a science materials center. Scientists and science educators from a local college or university can participate in the professional development program. Corporations also may offer in-kind support or provide a grant to get the science program started. Different kinds of community partnerships will be discussed in Chapter 9.

The five elements just described make up the "system" needed for building an effective elementary science program. More than 30 years of experience have shown that addressing only one or two of these elements—the science curriculum or professional development, for example—is not enough. All the elements are equally important and must be addressed simultaneously over a sustained period of time—at least five years—to ensure the institutionalization and long-term success of the program.

This comprehensive approach to the development and implementation of an inquiry-centered science program is called *systemic reform*. By viewing the science program as a system that is made of individual elements, all of which must be addressed simultaneously, school districts can create an environment where all students have an opportunity to learn and all teachers are supported in their teaching efforts.

**Building a
Foundation
for Change**

Key Points

▶ Creating an inquiry-centered classroom requires making significant changes in the way students learn and the way teachers teach.

▶ Five elements are central to the reform of elementary school science: an inquiry-centered science curriculum, professional development, science materials support, assessment, and administrative and community support. Although each element must be considered separately, they all must work together to create a new science education system.

For Further Reading

Beane, D. B. 1988. *Mathematics and Science: Critical Filters for the Future of Minority Students.* Washington, D.C.: The Mid-Atlantic Center for Race Equity.

Darling-Hammond, L. 1992. *Standards of Practice for Learner Centered Schools.* New York: National Center for Restructuring Schools and Learning.

Duckworth, E. 1987. *"The Having of Wonderful Ideas" and Other Essays on Teaching and Learning.* New York: Teachers College Press.

Fiske, E. B. 1992. *Smart Schools, Smart Kids.* New York: Simon & Schuster.

Goodlad, J. I. 1984. *A Place Called School.* New York: McGraw-Hill Book Company.

LeBuffe, J. R. 1994. *Hands-On Science in Elementary School.* Bloomington, Ind.: Phi Delta Kappa Educational Foundation.

Loucks-Horsley, S., R. Kapitan, M. D. Carlson, P. J. Kuerbis, R. C. Clark, G. M. Melle, T. P. Sachse, and E. Walton. 1990. *Elementary School Science for the '90s.* Andover, Mass.: The NETWORK, Inc., and Alexandria, Va.: Association for Supervision and Curriculum Development.

Marzano, R. J. 1992. *A Different Kind of Classroom: Teaching with Dimensions of Learning.* Alexandria, Va.: Association for Supervision and Curriculum Development.

National Research Council. 1996. *National Science Education Standards.* Washington, D.C.: National Academy Press.

Senge, P. M. 1990. *The Fifth Discipline: Mastering the Five Practices of Learning Organization.* New York: Doubleday.

Sigma Xi. 1994. *Scientists, Educators, and National Standards: Action at the Local Level.* Research Triangle Park, N.C.: Sigma Xi.

Planning for the New Elementary Science Program

4

It is a bad plan that admits of no modification.
— **Publilius Syrus, Maxim 469, circa 42 B.C.**

Planning is the process by which school districts determine how they are going to bring inquiry-centered science to their students. A structured planning process acts as a catalyst to change by focusing on the needs of students and teachers and the best ways of serving them. By planning carefully, school districts have a greater chance of successfully implementing the science program.

The planning process begins with people. As Robert Evans, an expert in strategic planning writes, "[Most people] treat reform as a product and, focusing on its structural frame, often overlook its human face. But change must be accomplished by people. . . . To do this, we must broaden our perspective on change and re-think the essentials of leadership."[1]

Getting Started: Identifying the Stakeholders

A core of committed people who are concerned about the status of science education in their district often band together to initiate a reform effort. They are sometimes called stakeholders, because they have a "stake" in the success of the program. Often the stakeholders are spurred on by a leader who has a vision of quality science education for all children and would like to see it become the districtwide norm. The planning process begins when the stakeholders come together to form a leadership team that will spearhead the reform.

Who are the stakeholders in a typical community? They may include the following:

Parents are an invaluable resource because they are invested in their children's education. Parents will work hard to create an improved science program if they are convinced that it's in their children's best interest. Some parents may bring to the reform effort expertise in a certain area, such as proposal writing. Parents may also serve as a link between the school and community organizations that can be enlisted to support science education reform.

Teachers have the job of nurturing children's natural curiosity and facilitating the inquiry-centered program. It's essential that they be included in discussions about the program and involved in decision making. At the start, many may not feel comfortable teaching inquiry-centered science. To cope with this situation, it's important to begin by identifying teachers who are familiar with inquiry-centered science and including them in the planning effort. This group of teachers can then work with those teachers who are less familiar with teaching through inquiry.

School administrators (principals and assistant principals) manage the school; their support is critical to the implementation of a new science program. Principals and their staff oversee teachers and provide opportunities for them to improve their teaching. Because principals work so closely with teachers, it's essential that principals understand all that is involved in teaching inquiry-centered science and be willing to support teachers in their efforts to develop expertise in this area. Principals may also be asked to explain, or even justify, the science program to parents, who view principals as their contact point in the schools. The more supportive principals are, the more likely the success of the reform effort.

The school district science coordinator or specialist coordinates all aspects of the science curriculum. These individuals are usually familiar with current research in science education, as well as with strategies for bringing about change in elementary science. In many school districts nationwide, science coordinators have spearheaded the reform effort.

The superintendent has tremendous influence over any district program. For example, each year he or she has the ability to allocate funds to initiate or expand the science program during the annual budget cycle. If the superintendent is convinced of the need for an inquiry-centered science program, success is likely. The superintendent is also in regular contact with the Board of Education and can take responsibility for keeping board members informed about the implementation process.

Members of the business community can form partnerships with school districts and assist with the reform effort by providing financial support for establishing a materials center or purchasing curriculum modules. They also may give interested employees time off from their job responsibilities so that they can assist school districts with their reform efforts.

Scientists and engineers from college and university faculties, industry, government laboratories, and science museums have a special interest in the scientific literacy of the next generation. They can help with the reform effort in many different ways, including assisting in professional development programs for teachers, reviewing curriculum materials, and becoming community advocates for the program.

Stakeholders may be spurred to action by many different factors. For example, parents, concerned about the quality of science teaching in their child's school, may bring this issue to the attention of other parents as well as to teachers and administrators. Or through experience, teachers may come to see that "learning through doing" is the most effective way to teach science. These like-minded teachers may begin talking to each other and to their principals, thus starting a chain reaction that results in the formation of a leadership team. In some cases, a superintendent may convene a task force to assess the status of the district's current science program. Finally, a university scientist or corporate leader, disappointed in the quality of recent graduates, may begin to work closely with local school districts to improve science teaching in

the schools. These and many other scenarios can initiate a major science education reform project.

Understanding the Risks of Change

Before proceeding to the next step in the planning process, it's important for leaders in the district to be aware that change is not accomplished without some controversy and dissent. Researchers have found that people go through at least six stages as they are introduced to an innovation and asked to participate in its execution.[2] Typically, people start out feeling detached and unconcerned about the proposed change. They then begin to want to know more about the change and become concerned about how it will affect them personally. More people may be willing to try the innovation at this stage, but they often feel unsure about the change and their ability to be successful at it. As time passes, an even greater number of people become committed to the effort and see themselves as important players.

At the beginning of a reform effort, people in the district will be at different stages of the change process. Some people may immediately recognize the importance of the project and be ready to be team players and collaborators. Other people may be more resistant to change and less interested in becoming involved; some people may even be opposed to the project. The leadership team should be prepared to accept this reality and to meet different stakeholders at a level where they feel comfortable. By knowing "who's who" in the district, the leader can set a realistic pace and bring on those who are ready first, while giving the others more time to become familiar with the innovation. In a process such as this, it's impossible to convince everyone that inquiry-centered science is worth pursuing. A more realistic goal is to bring in enough people who represent the stakeholders to create a "critical mass" of individuals dedicated to the reform.

Organizing the Leadership Team

In forming the leadership team, it's important that all the stakeholders be represented, but it's equally important that there be an appropriate balance of team members. An effective leadership team might consist of the school district science coordinator, the assistant superintendent for curriculum and instruction, an experienced elementary school teacher, an elementary school principal, and a scientist from the local community.

Although establishing a new science education program is a team effort, the team does need a strong leader. This person must be knowledgeable about elementary school science and how school bureaucracies operate. It's also helpful if the leader has a track record working in groups charged with building consensus around a shared vision. The ability to develop a vision and convey it to others is an essential quality of leadership. "Vision grabs," write Warren Bennis and Burt Nanus in their book *Leaders: The Strategies for Taking Charge.*[3] "Initially it grabs the leader, [who then is able to get the] attention [of] others [so that they] also get on the bandwagon." Furthermore, vision "animates, inspirits, transforms purpose into action." This kind of energy is essential to engage the leadership team in the complex planning process needed to put a new science program in place.

A Three-Step Strategic Planning Process

With the formation of a leadership team and the development of a shared vision, team members now must engage in an intensive strategic planning process. There is a growing body of literature about the planning process, and several useful sources are included at the end of this chapter. The essence of this process involves three steps.

1. Perform a needs assessment. This step consists of becoming informed about the status of the current science program in the district (i.e., the internal environment) and then about what is going on elsewhere and what resources are available (i.e., the external environment). Through the internal assessment, the district needs to focus on questions such as, How much inquiry-centered science is already going on in the district? Are teachers and administrators interested in pursuing inquiry-centered science? Have students been enthusiastic about inquiry-centered science? During the external assessment, the team should do extensive research on inquiry-centered science. Issues that need to be considered at this stage include what state frameworks are already in place, the National Science Education Standards, the kinds of curriculum modules available, opportunities for professional development programs, strategies for establishing a science materials support system, and opportunities for building support in the community. A subcommittee approach to the needs-assessment phase is described in the following section, "Planning Step by Step."

2. Articulate a districtwide vision for an effective science program. The committee must articulate a vision that reflects the unique values and beliefs of its district. The vision is the framework around which the reform effort is developed. The vision leads to goal statements, which are the foundation for the strategic plan. For example, a goal statement might be "Transform the teaching of science to communicate the excitement or relevance of science" or "Form collaborative and sustainable partnerships between school districts and local corporations." The goal statements provide a sense of direction and identify the discrepancies between where the district is and where it wants to be.

*Teachers, administrators, and community activists engage in the
strategic planning process, an essential step in ensuring the success
of an inquiry-centered science program.*

3. Produce a strategic plan. The strategic plan is a five-year plan for each of the five critical elements of a science program (i.e., curriculum, professional development, materials support, assessment, and administrative and community support). In addition to defining long-term goals, the plan identifies yearly targets for each element.

Planning Step by Step

To create a strategic plan, a school district must go through each phase of the strategic planning process for each element of its program. An effective way to proceed is to divide the leadership team into several subcommittees and to assign a chairperson for each group. Each chairperson has the responsibility of recruiting an additional five to seven people to serve on the subcommittee.

Each subcommittee's job is to develop a plan for its element, using the three-step strategic planning process described in the preceding section as a guide. As each subcommittee works, it's crucial that the whole committee meet regularly so that its members do not lose sight of the interdependent nature of their endeavor.

The following paragraphs describe each subcommittee's role in the planning process. These descriptions are meant to serve as examples of strategies that some school districts have found effective. The message implicit in each description is to proceed carefully. For example, most school districts do not start by purchasing a full set of science curriculum modules all at once; instead, they may begin by pilot testing one module per grade level. The teachers and the committee can then meet to review the results of these trials and make a joint decision about the logical next step. The same principle applies to the other four elements. As commitment to the program grows, so should investment in each of the program's distinctive elements.

Curriculum Subcommittee

The work of this subcommittee is twofold—to investigate the extent to which inquiry-centered science is currently being taught in the district and to identify curriculum materials that reflect the inquiry-centered philosophy. To find out what is going on in the district, subcommittee members may visit classrooms and contact principals. In the process, they may find teachers who are already teaching inquiry-centered science and would be interested in becoming involved in the reform effort. In this way, the leadership team can expand its base of support.

The next phase of this group's work, learning about the inquiry-centered materials that are available, is more complex and will probably take more time. The first step is for the subcommittee to become familiar with the National Science Education Standards and to consider how their goals align with local curriculum goals. From that point, there are many ways to look for available curriculum materials. For example, if the group knows of a district that already has an inquiry-centered science program in place, a few representatives could visit that district and observe classrooms, review curriculum materials, and meet with teachers and administrators familiar with inquiry-centered science.

In addition, several organizations, such as the National Science Resources Center (NSRC), the Education Development Center, and the Lawrence Hall of Science, can provide information about inquiry-centered science curriculum materials. (Information about these and other organizations can be found in Appendix A.)

After gathering this information and sharing it with the whole leadership team, the subcommittee might develop a *curriculum matrix*. The curriculum matrix is the framework for all that is taught in the science program. It's sometimes divided into subcategories, such as life science, earth science, physical science, and technology. The curriculum matrix should provide a sequence of learning within each category that enables students to build on previous learning and prepare them for subsequent explorations. The matrix for the NSRC's Science and Technology for Children (STC) program is shown in Figure 4-1.

As a way to begin developing the curriculum matrix, the subcommittee might decide to purchase a few sample modules and to pilot them in selected classrooms. This approach enables the subcommittee to offer the teachers it has identified as interested and informed during its initial research the opportunity to teach the modules and have some input into curriculum decisions. Figure 4-2 shows a sample sequence for the curriculum segment of the strategic plan.

Grade	Life, Earth, and Physical Sciences and Technology			
1	Organisms	Weather	Solids and Liquids	Comparing and Measuring
2	The Life Cycle of Butterflies	Soils	Changes	Balancing and Weighing
3	Plant Growth and Development	Rocks and Minerals	Chemical Tests	Sound
4	Animal Studies	Land and Water	Electric Circuits	Motion and Design
5	Microworlds	Ecosystems	Food Chemistry	Floating and Sinking
6	Experiments with Plants	Measuring Time	Magnets and Motors	The Technology of Paper

Sequence of STC Units

Figure 4-1. Curriculum matrix for the NSRC's Science and Technology for Children program

Professional Development Subcommittee

The first step for this group is to learn about the professional development program, sometimes called in-service education, for teachers currently in place in the district. How many days per teacher has the district allocated for in-service education? Is any time set aside specifically for science? Is there a way to incorporate the professional development needs for teaching science into the existing program? Has the group identified any principals who are particularly enthusiastic about the possibility of a new science program? If so, would any of them be willing to use some faculty meeting time for professional development purposes? Once the decision has been made to purchase some kits for pilot testing, this

Strategic Plan for Curriculum

	Year 1	Year 2	Year 3	Year 4	Year 5
Visit classrooms and principals.					
Identify interested and informed teachers.					
Identify available inquiry-centered curriculum materials.					
Visit classrooms in districts already implementing inquiry-centered science.					
Organize a curriculum committee to begin work on the district's curriculum matrix.					
Select teachers, resources, and grades for pilot testing.					
Conduct pilot testing.					
Review pilot results and make recommendations.					

Figure 4-2

subcommittee must ensure that time is allocated to prepare teachers adequately for introducing the new curriculum units.

Lack of sufficient time for professional development is an ongoing issue for inquiry-centered elementary science programs. Therefore, program directors need to be creative in finding ways to address the issue. For example, teachers could use the time they have while their students are attending art, music, or physical education for professional development efforts; arrange to have science when an experienced colleague can visit the class to assist; or invite parent volunteers to assist with materials management so that the teacher has more time to devote to working with students on substantive issues. Figure 4-3 shows a sample plan for the professional development element.

Strategic Plan for Professional Development

	Year 1	Year 2	Year 3	Year 4	Year 5
Become familiar with current professional development activities.					
Identify interested principals and lead teachers.					
Introduce staff to inquiry-centered science through formal and informal presentations.					
Coordinate professional development activities with pilot testing.					
Establish a short-term professional development plan.					
Identify outside sources for professional development opportunities.					
Establish a long-term professional development plan.					

Figure 4-3

Materials Support Subcommittee

This subcommittee has the responsibility of determining how to supply teachers with the materials they need to teach each of the modules in the science curriculum. This group will benefit greatly from a trip to an established science materials support center. Some of these science materials centers are consortia that serve more than one school district. If the district is near an established materials center, the subcommittee may want to consider creating a consortium.

The subcommittee can also seek help from local business and industry leaders in designing an effective science materials support center. For example, local engineers may be willing to evaluate the situation and develop a plan that meets the particular needs of the school district. Whatever approach is taken, it's crucial for school districts to begin thinking about materials support at the very beginning of the planning process and to be prepared to provide science materials to teachers on schedule, even at the pilot stage. Figure 4-4 shows a plan for this key element.

Strategic Plan for Science Materials Support	Year 1	Year 2	Year 3	Year 4	Year 5
Visit an established materials support center.					
Determine district's initial materials support needs.					
Consult with local business and industry leaders.					
Develop a long-term plan for effective science materials support.					

Figure 4-4

Assessment Subcommittee

Although new strategies for assessing student learning may not be introduced right away, it's important to begin thinking about assessment early in the planning process as preliminary decisions about curriculum are being made. Like the curriculum group, this subcommittee may want to find out whether anyone in the district is using alternative assessments, such as *performance-based assessments* or *portfolios* (a collection of student work viewed as samples of student learning) in any of the subject areas. Some teachers in the district may be knowledgeable about this subject and willing to share their expertise. It's essential that the assessment subcommittee remain in touch with the curriculum group and be familiar with the curriculum decisions that are being made.

Program assessment is as important as individual student assessment. Program managers must establish targets to ascertain whether the program is moving along on course. To accomplish this, program managers can design rubrics that chart where the program started (level 0) and where it is on the road to complete implementation (level 5). The rubrics are a way to assess the success of the program and to ensure that intermediate goals are met. Figure 4-5 outlines a sample plan for this element.

Administrative and Community Support Subcommittee

This subcommittee is charged with three tasks—developing a budget for the new science program, securing funds, and building awareness of the value of science reform within the school system and the community.

In developing the budget, the subcommittee needs to work with the school administrator responsible for budget planning. It should consider the following issues:

▶ The initial cost of science kits

▶ The costs of consumable materials needed to refurbish the kits

▶ Salaries for people who refurbish the kits

▶ Expenses associated with the ongoing professional development of teachers

4

Building a
Foundation
for Change

Strategic Plan for Assessment

	Year 1	Year 2	Year 3	Year 4	Year 5
Classroom Assessment					
Become familiar with performance-based approaches to science assessment.					
Identify teachers knowledgeable about alternative assessments.					
Conduct pilot testing with an emphasis on alternative assessments.					
Review results of pilot testing and make recommendations for incorporation into the districtwide assessment plan.					
Prepare teachers for implementation of districtwide plan.					
Program Assessment					
Establish rubrics for each element of the program.					
Use rubrics to ensure that target goals are met.					

Figure 4-5

Once initial financial estimates have been made, the subcommittee needs to consider funding sources. In some school districts, the superintendent can use some of the money set aside for textbooks to purchase science kits. School districts can apply to the U.S. Department of Education's Eisenhower Professional Development Program for funding for professional development activities.

Even with these options, however, most school districts find they need additional funds to establish and maintain an inquiry-centered science program. Therefore, it's important to forge partnerships with influential people in the community, such as corporate executives and university scientists. Corporate sponsors can offer their expertise in planning and organizing programs as well as financial assistance with certain parts of the program, such as the startup of the science materials center. Universities can make in-kind contributions, such as providing space for the science materials center.

Because community involvement will lead to a stronger program, this subcommittee would be wise to begin "spreading the word" about the program. One way to begin this effort is to have someone from this subcommittee make presentations at meetings of local business and civic organizations. Or someone may write an article for a local publication. Some school districts have found it helpful to hold a "Family Science Night," where the whole family comes to school and works on an inquiry-centered science activity together, in conjunction with a meeting of a local parent-teacher organization. Figure 4-6 shows a sample plan for this element of the program.

The Importance of Flexibility

As the district becomes more involved in reform, the planning team may find that it has to modify its original plans as a result of unforeseen circumstances. Flexibility is key. Although the plan provides a much-needed blueprint for action and a clear path to follow, it's impossible to understand all the variables until the program is actually in place.

Figure 4-7 (see pages 57-59) shows a completed strategic plan, with all of the five elements laid out on one chart. It shows clearly how the parts are connected and how many different activities are taking place simultaneously.

Strategic Plan for
Administrative and Community Support

	Year 1	Year 2	Year 3	Year 4	Year 5
Budget Issues					
Establish a budget for the program considering the following:					
— Initial cost of science kits					
— Costs of refurbishing kit					
— Salaries for refurbishing staff					
— Expenses for professional development					
Consider additional funding sources.					
Networking Activities					
Make presentations at local business and civic organizations.					
Hold a Family Science Night in conjunction with the local parent-teacher organization.					
Begin forging partnerships with business leaders and university scientists.					
Establish multiple partnerships with stakeholders.					

Figure 4-6

The Power of the Committee

The Hinsdale School District in Illinois discovered that the inspiration provided by a committed science supervisor and her science committee was indeed what it took to bring inquiry-centered science to its students.

Here's how it happened. Mary Kelly, science supervisor for the district, became interested in inquiry-centered science in the early 1980s after studying some of the recent research about how children learn. She brought this information to the attention of some of the principals in the district and the superintendent, who encouraged Kelly to identify some school districts that had put these ideas into practice. Kelly got in touch with Emma Walton, then science supervisor in Anchorage, Alaska, and Larry Small of the neighboring Schaumburg School District in Illinois. Her discussions with Walton and Small helped Kelly realize the value of using science kits as the basis for the inquiry-centered science program. With their encouragement, Kelly found the courage to consider abandoning textbooks altogether in favor of a modular, kit-based program.

But there were obstacles to overcome. The school board saw no reason to make any changes, because the district's test scores were fine. At that point, Kelly called together a committee of scientists to help promote the idea of an inquiry-centered science program. Scientists know that offering children inquiry-centered experiences at an early age increases the probability that their interest in science will be sustained throughout school. As it turned out, the support of the scientific community was the added spark needed to convince the school board to try something new.

At this juncture, Kelly faced a roadblock that school districts embarking on reform today don't have to confront—a shortage of high-quality curriculum materials. In the early 1980s, there were few science modules available for elementary schools. So for Kelly to realize her dream, she and her district had to begin to develop the modules themselves.

continued on next page

4

Building a
Foundation
for Change

The Power of the Committee *continued*

"We began writing the modules and setting up a centralized materials center," recalls Kelly. "We phased in the program over a period of four years. We now have four modules in place for each grade [K–6]. I conduct the teacher training program for all the teachers using these curriculum materials."

Although Hinsdale continues to use the modules they developed and wrote, most educators advise school districts not to embark on this time-consuming, difficult endeavor. Fortunately, districts can instead use one of several commercial curriculum projects that are consonant with the National Science Education Standards.

Over the past several years, Hinsdale's program has reached out to neighboring districts; now 10 districts use the science modules and receive supplies from the Hinsdale materials center. "It has proven more cost-effective for districts to join us rather than start their own programs," says Kelly.

Although Hinsdale has a successful program in place, Kelly knows her work is not done. "The science committee is active again," says Kelly. "Our next goal is working on staff development so that teachers can develop more sophisticated techniques to use in inquiry-centered classrooms."

Strategic Plan for the
Elementary Science Program

	Year 1	Year 2	Year 3	Year 4	Year 5
Curriculum					
Visit classrooms and principals.					
Identify interested and informed teachers.					
Identify available inquiry-centered curriculum materials.					
Visit classrooms in districts already implementing inquiry-centered science.					
Organize a curriculum committee to begin work on the district's curriculum matrix.					
Select teachers, resources, and grades for pilot testing.					
Conduct pilot testing.					
Review pilot results and make recommendations.					
Professional Development					
Become familiar with current professional development activities.					
Identify interested principals and lead teachers.					
Introduce staff to inquiry-centered science through formal and informal presentations.					
Coordinate professional development activities with pilot testing.					

Figure 4-7

continued on next page

Strategic Plan for the Elementary Science Program *continued*

	Year 1	Year 2	Year 3	Year 4	Year 5
Establish a short-term professional development plan.					
Identify outside sources for professional development opportunities.					
Establish a long-term professional development plan.					
Science Materials Support					
Visit an established materials support center.					
Determine district's initial materials support needs.					
Consult with local business and industry leaders.					
Develop a long-term plan for effective science materials support.					
Assessment					
Classroom Assessment					
Become familiar with performance-based approaches to science assessment.					
Identify teachers knowledgeable about alternative assessments.					
Conduct pilot testing with an emphasis on alternative assessments.					

	Year 1	Year 2	Year 3	Year 4	Year 5
Review results of pilot testing and make recommendations for incorporation into the districtwide assessment plan.					
Prepare teachers for implementation of districtwide plan.					
Program Assessment Establish rubrics for each element of the program.					
Use rubrics to ensure that target goals are met.					
Administrative and Community Support **Budget Issues** Establish a budget for the program considering the following: — Initial cost of science kits — Costs of refurbishing kits — Salaries for refurbishing staff — Expenses for professional development					
Consider additional funding sources.					
Networking Activities Make presentations at local business and civic organizations.					
Hold a Family Science Night in conjunction with the local parent-teacher organization.					
Begin forging partnerships with business leaders and university scientists.					
Establish multiple partnerships with stakeholders.					

4

Building a
Foundation
for Change

Key Points

▶ To implement an inquiry-centered elementary science program, it is crucial to engage in a step-by-step strategic planning process for each element of the science program.

▶ One of the first steps of the planning process is forming a leadership team consisting of a school district science coordinator, the assistant superintendent for curriculum and instruction, an experienced elementary school teacher, an elementary school principal, and a scientist from the local community.

▶ A strong leader who has the skills to build consensus and articulate the team vision can spur the leadership team to action.

▶ The leadership team needs to be aware that most people find change difficult. Furthermore, people in the district will be at different stages of the change process, a factor that must be taken into account in setting a time frame for implementing the reform.

▶ The result of the planning process is a sample plan for each element and for the whole program. As school districts gain more knowledge, they may find it necessary to modify their initial plans.

For Further Reading

Bennis, W., and B. Nanus. 1985. *Leaders: The Strategies for Taking Charge*. New York: HarperPerennial.

Evans, R. 1993. "The Human Face of Reform." *Educational Leadership* 51: 19-23.

Gardner, H. 1995. "Limited Visions, Limited Means: Two Obstacles to Meaningful Education Reform." *Daedalus, Journal of the American Academy of Arts and Sciences* 124: 101-05.

Hord, S. M., W. L. Rutherford, L. Huling-Austin, and G. E. Hall. 1987. *Taking Charge of Change*. Alexandria, Va.: Association of Supervision and Curriculum Development.

LeBuffe, J. R. 1994. *Hands-on Science in Elementary School*. Bloomington, Ind.: Phi Delta Kappa Educational Foundation.

National Research Council. 1993. *A Nationwide Education Support System for Teachers and Schools*. Washington, D.C.: National Academy Press.

Schlechty, P. C. 1990. *Schools for the Twenty-first Century: Leadership Imperatives for Educational Reform*. San Francisco: Jossey-Bass.

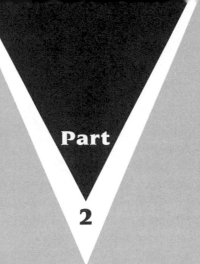

Part

2

The Nuts and Bolts of Change

Criteria for Selecting Inquiry-Centered Science Curriculum Materials

In schools—including good schools—all over the world, we have come to accept certain performances as signals of knowledge or understanding. If you answer questions on a multiple-choice test in a certain way, or carry out a problem set in a specified manner, you will be credited with understanding. No one ever asks the question, "But do you really understand?"

— **Howard Gardner, The Unschooled Mind, 1991**

School districts throughout the country observe a unique tradition every few years: the review and selection of curriculum materials. The science materials adoption committee, charged with the task of reviewing elementary science curriculum materials, invites publishers to submit their materials for consideration. Some publishers respond by supplying sets of attractively illustrated, full-color elementary textbooks, sometimes with optional videotapes, videodisks, or computer software. Other publishers offer a very different kind of elementary science program: a series of inquiry-centered science modules. The modular nature of these materials allows teachers or school districts to build their own unique curriculum by using a combination of modules from one or more of the different programs available.

How can the science materials adoption committee choose among all these different products? Are there any guidelines that the committee can use to make this job easier?

The purpose of this chapter is to present three sets of well-tested criteria that materials adoption committees can use as they review elementary science curriculum materials. The first set concerns *pedagogical appropriateness.* This category encompasses the following key questions: 1) Do the materials address the important goals of elementary science teaching and learning? 2) Are inquiry and activity the basis of learning experiences? 3) Are the instructional approaches consonant with the goals of the program?

The second set includes information about *science content.* Criteria in this category cover whether the materials are scientifically accurate and whether they are developmentally appropriate. The third set concerns *presentation of information and format.* These criteria refer to the clarity of the information and how it is presented in the written materials. All three sets of criteria are based on a chart used for reviewing curriculum materials developed by the National Science Resources Center, which is presented at the end of this chapter. These criteria are consistent with the National Science Education Standards. The following sections explain the criteria included on this chart.

Criteria for Judging Pedagogical Appropriateness

Pedagogical appropriateness is a broad subject, covering many aspects of teaching. This discussion emphasizes three areas: addressing the goals of elementary science teaching and learning, focusing on inquiry and activity as the basis of learning experiences, and using an effective instructional approach.

Addressing the Goals of Elementary Science Teaching and Learning

1. Do the materials focus on concrete experiences with science phenomena? As discussed in Chapters 1 and 2, building students' conceptual understanding requires ample opportunity for students

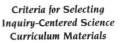

A teacher uses a criteria checklist to evaluate an inquiry-centered science module.

to work directly with science phenomena. Through hands-on, inquiry-centered experiences, students build their knowledge base.

2. Do the materials enable children to investigate important science concepts in depth over an extended period of time? The materials should give students an opportunity to study a single subject and its related concepts in depth. For example, in a 16-lesson module about butterflies, key concepts will include the life cycle of a butterfly and its stages. Furthermore, teachers need to teach lessons from the science module at least two times a week for six to eight weeks, depending on the grade level, to achieve the appropriate level of depth.

3. Do the curriculum materials contribute to the development of scientific reasoning and problem-solving skills? If the materials are to accomplish this goal, process skills must be introduced in a logical and developmentally appropriate progression. For example, in the early primary grades (grades 1 and 2), children benefit from focusing on observing, measuring, and identifying properties of concrete objects and organisms, such as butterflies, or of easily observable phenomena, such as weather. In grades 3 through 5, children can begin to deal with more complex phenomena, such as electricity, and learn to seek evidence and recognize patterns and cycles. By the time children reach grade 6, they are ready to begin designing their own controlled experiments.

4. Do the materials stimulate students' interest and relate science learning to daily life? Science programs should help students become more acute observers of their world, better able to understand phenomena and to identify patterns. For example, students may begin to realize that the caterpillars crawling in their back yard in spring are part of the life cycle of butterflies. In making these connections, students are well on their way to seeing and appreciating the relevance of science to everyday life.

To stimulate this kind of interest, the science program should make an explicit effort to include materials students find intrinsically interesting, as well as questions students can investigate on their own. Then, students may choose to read a book on the subject or perform a home science activity.

5. Do the materials build conceptual understanding over several lessons through a logical sequence of related activities? To build conceptual understanding, the curriculum materials must have a well-defined, logical story line and engage students in activities that build on one another in a related sequence. For example, in the second-grade Full Option Science System (FOSS) module *Pebbles, Sand, and Silt,* students begin their study of earth materials by investigating the properties of rocks. Then, they explore a specific kind of rock—river rock—that contains earth materials of different sizes. Next, students investigate how people use earth materials to construct objects; they make rubbings from sandpaper, sculptures from sand, jewelry from clay, and bricks from clay soil. The module concludes with an investigation of soil, which is made of the earth materials students have already investigated.

In addition, as children mature, the amount of information they are expected to master, as well as its complexity, should increase. The curriculum matrix, the framework for the science program, will tell the committee whether the program is designed in this way. For example, in the Science and Technology for Children (STC) program, children study *Electric Circuits* in fourth grade and *Magnets and Motors* in sixth grade. The fourth-grade module focuses on the basic principles of electricity, while the sixth-grade module shows how electricity and magnetism work together in a motor. Providing children with a working knowledge of electricity before they begin *Magnets and Motors* allows them to expand their knowledge and reach for a higher level of understanding as they grow older.

6. Does the instructional sequence include opportunities to assess children's prior knowledge and experience? An effective way to ensure that this issue is being considered is to look for evidence of the learning cycle in the program. As discussed in Chapter 2, the learning cycle encourages students to *focus, explore, reflect,* and *apply* as they study science. During the focus stage, students have an opportunity to share what they already know about a subject and what they would like to learn. Students' responses will inform the teacher of the students' prior knowledge and experience and about whether they have misconceptions or particular interests that need to be addressed. In many curriculum programs, there are opportunities to refer to students' prior knowledge as they progress through the learning module.

Focusing on Inquiry and Activity as the Basis of Learning Experiences

1. Does the material focus on student inquiry and engage students in the processes of science? While students are working on inquiry-centered activities, the processes of science should be evident. Examples of these processes include observing and recognizing noticeable changes in objects or phenomena, grouping objects by their properties, making scale drawings, making predictions, and drawing conclusions from data.

2. Does the material provide opportunities for students to gather and defend their own evidence and express their results in a variety of ways? Young children can gather evidence through observations, and they can defend their observations verbally, in writing, in drawings, through simple graphs, or through dramatic presentations. Students in fifth and sixth grade have opportunities to engage in these activities as they begin planning and designing their own investigations. Older children should continue to have the option of expressing their results in a variety of ways—by making graphs or tables, through expository writing, or by developing dramatic presentations, for example.

Using an Effective Instructional Approach

1. Does the material include a balance of student-directed and teacher-facilitated activities as well as discussions? The committee should look for evidence that both student-directed and teacher-facilitated activities are part of the program. Both approaches are important, because students need opportunities not only to pursue their own interests but also to learn concepts with the help of the teacher. Effective programs offer time for individual and small-group explorations of science phenomena, as well as for explorations and discussions guided by the teacher to ensure that students have certain basic experiences and that knowledge is being synthesized and understood.

2. Does the material incorporate effective strategies for the teacher and/or students to use in assessing student learning? As will be seen in Chapter 8, assessments in inquiry-centered science programs differ from those in traditional ones because they stress the importance of using a variety of assessments. For example, students may perform activities similar to those done in the module, complete a writing assignment, or complete a paper-and-pencil test to demonstrate what they have learned. These different kinds of assessments provide teachers with ample information about what students learned during the module and whether learning goals were met.

3. Does the teacher's guide suggest opportunities for integrating science with other areas of the curriculum? Science should be integrated with other areas of the curriculum. During the kindergarten and first-grade Insights module *Living Things,* for example, children observe plants and animals both outdoors and in a classroom plant terrarium and then write stories about their experiences, read books about terraria, and draw pictures of the trees they observe. These activities connect science to language arts and art. In a fifth-grade FOSS module entitled *Variables,* students apply mathematics skills to science by graphing the number of swings a pendulum will make in a unit of time. In a second- and third-grade Insights module entitled *Liquids,* the teacher may invite a Red Cross worker, a nurse, or an emergency medical technician to the class to talk about drinkable, nondrinkable, and poisonous liquids, which creates a link to social studies.

4. Do students have opportunities to work collaboratively and alone? Corporate leaders have stressed the importance of teaching young people how to work in a team and to make decisions by consensus. For example, in the STC unit *Balancing and Weighing*, second-graders work in pairs as they explore the relationship between balance and weight. Teamwork allows students to learn group problem-solving strategies and to work with members of the class they might not normally seek out. After numerous experiences working together, students then work individually to construct a mobile. This activity provides students with time to better understand the concepts.

Criteria for Judging Science Content

The following criteria address content issues that need to be considered by the science materials adoption committee.

1. Is the science content current and accurately represented? To be useful, the scientific information in the program must be accurate and reflect current scientific knowledge.

2. Does the content emphasize scientific inquiry? The vision presented in the *National Science Education Standards* requires that students engage in scientific inquiry to develop their understanding of science concepts. Evidence of scientific inquiry includes "opportunities for students to ask questions, plan and conduct investigations, use appropriate tools and techniques to gather data, think critically and logically to develop explanations based on what they have observed, construct and analyze alternative explanations, and communicate scientific arguments."[1]

3. Is the content of the science program consistent with the National Science Education Standards? The Standards specify the knowledge and skills children at various levels should acquire in physical science, life science, and earth and space science. They also include information about what children should know in the areas of science and technology and of the history and nature of science. Finally, the Standards include information about how students can learn to use scientific knowledge to make informed decisions.

4. Does the background material for teachers address the science content that is taught, as well as common misconceptions? The material should include the major points the teacher needs to know to teach the lesson and should address common misconceptions. For example, many students think that because oil is viscous, it also must be dense, but this is not the case. Such misconceptions must be addressed in the materials so that teachers know how to deal with these issues when they come up in class.

5. Is the treatment of content appropriate for the grade level? Developmental appropriateness is an important issue that must be addressed in evaluating elementary science materials. Both the depth of treatment and the content must be appropriate for each grade. For example, third-graders can observe the life cycle of plants, but they are generally not yet ready to design controlled experiments to test the variables that affect plant growth. That level of complexity is more appropriate for sixth-graders. Similarly, second-graders can understand that cars move fast or slowly, but they are not ready to understand acceleration and Newton's Laws of Motion.

6. Is the content free of bias? The information presented in the program should reflect different viewpoints and avoid personal opinions and biases. If there are several sides to societal issues involving science and technology, all perspectives should be addressed.

7. Is the writing style for students and teachers interesting and engaging, and is scientific language used appropriately? Any subject becomes more interesting when it is well-written, and science is no exception. Students will develop a deeper understanding of a subject if the language is engaging and if scientific language is used appropriately.

8. Is scientific vocabulary used to facilitate understanding rather than as an end in itself? Learning scientific terms out of context does not help students understand science. If these terms are put into a context, defined accurately and appropriately, and used consistently, however, students will be able to understand them.

9. Is science represented as an enterprise connected to society? Opportunities for students to relate science to the real world enhance their understanding of social issues. For example, as scientists raise concerns about global warming and other environmental issues, it is important for students to be knowledgeable about the underlying scientific concepts.

Criteria for Judging Presentation and Format
The following criteria address issues related to the presentation and format of the material.

1. Are the print materials for students well-written, develop-

mentally appropriate, and compelling in content? The committee needs to assess whether the materials are written at the right level for the designated grade and are interesting and informative for children.

2. Are the directions for implementing activities clear in both the teacher's guide and student materials? For example, the instructions should include step-by-step directions that are accurate and easy to follow, suggestions for time limits, and the proper safety precautions.

3. Are the suggestions for instructional delivery in the teacher's guide adequate? The curriculum materials should include information related to procedural techniques. For example, do the instructions provide detailed information about the best way to pour liquids or mix solids? Are instructions about the best way to use a hand lens explained in both words and pictures? This information helps ensure that the students will get accurate results after they complete the experiment or investigation.

4. Are the materials free of ethnic, cultural, racial, economic, age, and gender bias? Indications that these issues have been addressed include pictures and photographs of children of different ethnic backgrounds, frequent references to the active involvement of girls in science investigations, and acknowledgment of the cultural diversity that can be found in many classrooms nationwide.

5. Are appropriate strategies provided to meet the special needs of diverse populations? The curriculum materials should acknowledge the validity of different learning styles and include different kinds of learning activities, such as those that emphasize visual learning, auditory learning, and tactile learning. In addition, the materials must take into consideration students with physical disabilities and those with limited proficiency in English.

6. Are lists of materials for each activity provided, as well as a complete set of materials and information about reasonably priced replacement materials? Teachers cannot teach hands-on science curriculum units without adequate materials. Therefore, it is essential that the necessary materials be easily obtained and that the modules include information about ordering replacement materials.

7. Are safety precautions included where needed? Attention to safety issues is imperative. For example, if students are going to be working with chemicals or heat, the use of goggles should be included in the directions and any accompanying pictures.

8. Are instructions for using laboratory equipment and materials clear and adequate? Clear and precise instructions for using scientific equipment will ensure successful lessons, especially for teachers new to hands-on science teaching. The instructions also should include necessary safety precautions.

Using the Criteria

Curriculum materials committees often find it useful to convert criteria such as those discussed above into a checklist. The advantage of a checklist is that at a glance, reviewers can tell what they should be looking for.

Figure 5-1 shows how the criteria discussed in this chapter can be converted into an easy-to-use checklist for reviewers. A tool such as this one can make the job of reviewing materials and making decisions about them much easier.

Criteria for Judging Inquiry-Centered Science Curriculum Materials

Criteria for Judging Pedagogical Appropriateness

Addressing the Goals of Elementary Science Teaching and Learning

1. Do the materials focus on concrete experiences with science phenomena?

2. Do the materials enable children to investigate important science concepts in depth over an extended period of time?

3. Do the curriculum materials contribute to the development of scientific reasoning and problem-solving skills?

4. Do the materials stimulate students' interest and relate science learning to daily life?

5. Do the materials build conceptual understanding over several lessons through a logical sequence of related activities?

6. Does the instructional sequence include opportunities to assess children's prior knowledge and experience?

Focusing on Inquiry and Activity as the Basis of Learning Experiences

1. Does the material focus on student inquiry and engage students in the processes of science?

2. Does the material provide opportunities for students to gather and defend their own evidence and express their results in a variety of ways?

Using an Effective Instructional Approach

1. Does the material include a balance of student-directed and teacher-facilitated activities as well as discussions?

2. Does the material incorporate effective strategies for the teacher and/or students to use in assessing student learning?

3. Does the teacher's guide suggest opportunities for integrating science with other areas of the curriculum?

4. Do students have opportunities to work collaboratively and alone?

Figure 5-1

continued on next page

Criteria for Judging Inquiry-Centered Science Curriculum Materials *continued*

Criteria for Judging Science Content

1. Is the science content current and accurately represented?

2. Does the content emphasize scientific inquiry?

3. Is the content of the science program consistent with the National Science Education Standards?

4. Does the background material for teachers address the science content that is taught, as well as common misconceptions?

5. Is the treatment of content appropriate for the grade level?

6. Is the content free of bias?

7. Is the writing style for students and teachers interesting and engaging, and is scientific language used appropriately?

8. Is scientific vocabulary used to facilitate understanding rather than as an end in itself?

9. Is science represented as an enterprise connected to society?

Criteria for Judging Presentation and Format

1. Are the print materials for students well-written, developmentally appropriate, and compelling in content?

2. Are the directions for implementing activities clear in both the teacher's guide and student materials?

3. Are the suggestions for instructional delivery in the teacher's guide adequate?

4. Are the materials free of ethnic, cultural, racial, economic, age, and gender bias?

5. Are appropriate strategies provided to meet the special needs of diverse populations?

6. Are lists of materials for each activity provided, as well as a complete set of materials and information about reasonably priced replacement materials?

7. Are safety precautions included where needed?

8. Are instructions for using laboratory equipment and materials clear and adequate?

Key Points

▶ Three sets of criteria are useful in evaluating elementary science curriculum materials. The first set concerns pedagogical appropriateness, which encompasses strategies for building conceptual understanding, teaching science as inquiry, and applying effective instructional strategies. The second set concerns science content, and the third, presentation and format.

▶ The curriculum materials should be consistent with the National Science Education Standards.

▶ Converting criteria into a checklist for reviewers is an effective way to evaluate curriculum materials and make sound curriculum decisions.

For Further Reading

Brooks, J. G., and M. G. Brooks. 1993. *In Search of Understanding: The Case for Constructivist Classrooms.* Alexandria, Va.: Association for Supervision and Curriculum Development.

Bybee, R. W., and J. D. McInerney, eds. 1995. *Redesigning the Curriculum.* Colorado Springs: BSCS.

Champagne, A. B., and L. E. Hornig, eds. 1987. *This Year in School Science 1986: The Science Curriculum.* Washington, D.C.: American Association for the Advancement of Science.

Gardner, H. 1991. *The Unschooled Mind.* New York: BasicBooks.

Glatthorn, A. A. 1994. *Developing a Quality Curriculum.* Alexandria, Va.: Association for Supervision and Curriculum Development.

Harlen, W. S. 1989. *Developing Science in the Primary Classroom.* Portsmouth, N.H.: Heinemann Educational Books, Inc.

Loucks-Horsley, S., R. Kapitan, M. D. Carlson, P. J. Kuerbis, R. C. Clark, G. M. Melle, T. P. Sachse, and E. Walton. 1990. *Elementary School Science for the '90s.* Andover, Mass.: The NETWORK, Inc., and Alexandria, Va.: Association for Supervision and Curriculum Development.

Marzano, R. J. 1992. *A Different Kind of Classroom: Teaching with Dimensions of Learning.* Alexandria, Va.: Association for Supervision and Curriculum Development.

National Research Council. 1996. *National Science Education Standards.* Washington, D.C.: National Academy Press.

National Science Resources Center. 1996. *Resources for Teaching Elementary School Science.* Washington, D.C.: National Academy Press.

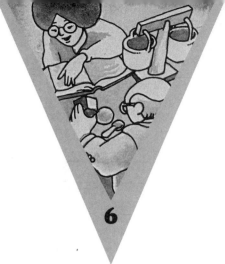

6

Professional Development for Inquiry-Centered Science

If teachers are given choices—are allowed to make decisions—are, in short, treated as both professionals and human beings—better teaching and better programs result. . . . When teachers are not "locked" into programs—are not tied into textbook-structured courses of study—their classrooms are alive and stimulating.
— **Ronald B. Jackson,** *Something of Value,* **1973**

$\mathbf{W}$ith the curriculum selection process under way, it is time for the district to begin to organize the professional development component of the program. The initial goal of professional development is to introduce teachers to inquiry-centered science teaching and familiarize them with the specific science modules they will be teaching. This can be accomplished most effectively by creating a collegial environment in which teachers feel comfortable sharing ideas and working closely with experienced teachers.

These don't sound like revolutionary ideas, but in fact they challenge some basic premises on which the American public school system is based. Traditionally, teachers have been assigned a classroom and have taught their students alone, conferring with few people and making their own decisions about how to implement the curriculum. Many teachers have become accustomed to this autonomy, and some even equate it with professionalism.

Carl Glickman calls this situation the "one-room school" syndrome, the tradition of isolationism created back in the days when teachers literally worked alone in their schoolhouses without any contact with other teachers. This tradition has lingered, and it manifests itself in today's schools by the tendency not to "connect staff for purposes of sharing expertise, solving problems, and pursuing improvement."[1] Given this context, a second, long-term goal of professional development is to foster the development of an environment in which teachers can learn and grow professionally.

This chapter discusses strategies that can be used to achieve these two goals. The chapter begins with a discussion of the characteristics of effective professional development programs for all teachers, from the novice to those in the "competent" stage to expert teachers. It concludes with a discussion of some strategies for professional development that have been successful in school districts throughout the country.

Characteristics of an Effective Professional Development Program

The *National Science Education Standards* includes as part of its vision for science education reform increased opportunities for teachers to grow professionally throughout their careers. According to the *Standards*, "Teachers should have opportunities for structured reflection on their teaching practice with colleagues, for collaborative curriculum planning, and for active participation in professional teaching and scientific networks. The challenge of professional development for teachers is to create optimal collaborative learning situations in which the best sources of expertise are linked with the experiences and current needs of the teachers."[2]

Research and experience have shown that an effective way to introduce teachers to an inquiry-centered curriculum is to have them experience each module in much the same way their students will. This approach is based on the assumption that the constructivist learning model is valid for adults as well as for children. Through the experience of working with the materials, discovering how the investigations build on one another, and encountering their own difficulties with the equipment or the concepts, teachers not only prepare themselves to teach the module but also realize that they can learn along with their students. Teachers who have made this discovery begin to rethink their role in the classroom and view themselves less as lecturers and more as learning facilitators.

The following list highlights strategies that have been effective in helping school districts create innovative professional development programs. These strategies will also help districts achieve the goals outlined in the *Standards*.

1. Provide continuous and sustained support for professional development. School district administrators need to send a clear message of support to teachers. The support must go beyond rhetoric and take the form of stressing science as a basic in the school curriculum and of providing teachers with a "safety net" so that they have time to grow professionally. Teachers should have the opportunity to experiment with different teaching strategies and to make mistakes without fear of consequences, with administrators recognizing that this is an essential part of their personal learning process. This learning process is not smooth, and nobody will become an expert overnight. Teachers need to have time to reflect on the new ideas that are being introduced and to assimilate them at their own pace. They also need to be aware that because science is considered a basic, they will be evaluated for their science teaching.

Other forms of support include providing teachers with the necessary materials on time, offering graduate credit for attending professional development classes, verbally praising teachers' accomplishments, and publishing their achievements in school publications and the local media.

2. Provide teachers with time to engage in professional development activities. It is crucial that administrators recognize the key role teachers play in implementing a science program and give them the time they need to become proficient. This means granting teachers time to participate in professional development activities during the school day. Unfortunately, given the way time is organized in the schools, this is no easy task.

Program directors and teachers need to be creative in the ways they address this issue. For example, teachers could use the time they have while their students are attending art, music, or physical education classes for their own professional development; arrange to have science when an experienced colleague could visit the class to assist; or invite parent volunteers to help with materials management so that the teacher has more time to devote to working with students on substantive issues. Other strategies include communicating electronically with other teachers to discuss science teaching strategies and encouraging students to assist with materials management so that the teacher can work with other students who have questions or need special help.

Teachers also have to be aware that involvement in the science program may require them to make additional time commitments. For example, they may need to attend summer institutes or after-school meetings. The incentive to give extra time will be greater if teachers see the administration working hard to make the school day more flexible to accommodate effective science instruction.

3. Create an environment of collegiality and collaboration. Teachers can benefit tremendously from professional relationships that enable them to feel comfortable sharing ideas, acknowledging difficulties, and solving problems they encounter in the classroom. Although a certain amount of discussion usually takes place informally among teachers, the best way to foster professional relationships is to institute some formal ways for teachers to interact. In formalizing such discussions, it is crucial that experienced teachers assume a leadership role. Discussions can wander unless leaders are present to facilitate them. One obvious way to formalize discussions is to address issues related to inquiry-centered science teaching at faculty meetings. For example, in Huntsville, Alabama, teachers found that their discussions during faculty meetings helped enhance relationships among teachers, making these meetings richer learning experiences.

Many districts have ensured that there will be opportunities for teachers to share experiences by scheduling at least two meetings each semester where they can discuss their progress in imple-

*Teachers and a scientist (right) collaborate to construct a motor
during a workshop on a sixth-grade module.*

menting inquiry-centered science modules. Such meetings help
new or inexperienced teachers become more comfortable sharing
problems and better able to accept guidance from their more experienced colleagues.

**4. Incorporate the change process into the professional de-
velopment design.** In Chapter 4, we explained the stages that
stakeholders typically go through as they become familiar with an
innovation. Teachers undergo similar stages. For example, their
initial reaction may be indifference to the innovation; this is followed by a concern about how it is going to affect them personally. As their familiarity with the program grows, teachers become
more invested in the program and more interested in learning
how to use it comfortably. At the final stage, teachers are concerned primarily with how the new program is affecting their students and with developing strategies to make the program even
more effective.

Those responsible for designing the staff development program need to be aware of these stages and of the position of their teachers on the continuum of change. For example, if teachers in a particular district are at the "indifferent" stage, the emphasis of the professional development program should be on familiarizing them with the goals of inquiry-centered science. If teachers are concerned about who will be responsible for collecting the materials needed for the lessons, program designers need to address this issue and suggest how the materials will be provided and managed.

In most districts, teachers will be at different places along the continuum. Some teachers may already be comfortable teaching inquiry-centered science, while others may be afraid even to open the kit. In situations like this, districts may consider "pairing" a more experienced teacher with a less experienced one. This approach has been used in the East Baton Rouge Parish Public School System; experience there has shown that pairing increases the confidence and comfort level of the less experienced teacher.

Initiating Professional Development at the Right Time in the Right Way

Using the strategies mentioned above as a guide, the district must next consider when to begin the professional development program, who should be involved in the planning, and at what level of professional development to aim the program. The best time to develop a professional development program is usually during the six months before inquiry-centered modules are introduced in the district. As part of the professional development plan, the school district needs to determine how many schools are going to be phased in over a five-year period, and at what pace. Most districts have found that it is better to start with the teachers in a limited number of elementary schools and then to add more schools in each subsequent year. Depending on the size of the district, it takes between three and five years to introduce all the elementary school teachers in the district to all the science modules and for teachers to become reasonably comfortable teaching science through inquiry. In addition, fine-tuning pedagogical techniques, learning more science content, and integrating the science module with other areas of the curriculum are issues that need to be a continuing part of the teachers' lifelong professional development.

The time frame for introducing the professional development program is a complex issue related to the size of the district, the level of resources available, and the current capacity of the district. All these factors must be taken into consideration so that districts realize their long-term goal: to establish an effective, thoughtful, and comprehensive professional development program. Pressure to complete implementation should not interfere with realizing this goal.

It's also important to ensure that teachers become involved in the planning of the professional development program and that they become key players in the decision-making process. By making teachers partners in the planning process, administrators can go a long way toward building trust and creating a collegial atmosphere in which all participants acknowledge that they have much to learn from each other.

Levels of Professional Development

In designing an effective professional development program, it's important to understand the phases that teachers typically undergo in their journey to become highly experienced elementary science teachers and the kinds of professional development programs appropriate for each phase. Research has shown that most teachers go through at least three phases: novice, competent, and expert.[3] The three programs described below are tailored for each of these phases.

Phase I: The Introductory Program

An effective professional development program for novice teachers begins with an intensive introduction to inquiry-centered science, often in the form of a two- or four-week institute held the summer before the new curriculum is scheduled to be introduced in the classroom. At the institute, teachers become familiar with the science modules they will be teaching during the first six months (usually one or two modules) and discuss basic issues, such as managing the materials and organizing the lesson so that it can be completed in a timely fashion. In a relaxed setting with their peers, teachers can share common concerns, including the likelihood of increased noise in the classroom and how to relinquish a little control and let the children pursue their own interests during the science lesson. Teachers can help students pursue their own interests by providing them with opportunities to work independently. For some teachers, encouraging independent work may create a new set of challenges about how to maintain order in the classroom.

Teachers new to inquiry-centered science are especially concerned about classroom management issues such as these, because one of the greatest challenges of teaching science through inquiry is creating an environment conducive to interactive learning. How, many teachers wonder, does one create a setting where children feel challenged, eager to ask questions, and ready to explore their ideas with their classmates? Experienced teachers have found that establishing rules carefully is key; children must understand that they can talk but not shout, that accidents with the materials may happen but they should try to be careful, and that although they will be working independently or in groups, they must be prepared to listen to the teacher at appropriate times.

It's hard for many teachers to give up their traditional ideas of an orderly classroom. Consequently, even after attending an initial institute, teachers tend to revert to their old teaching strategies. They may be reluctant to divide the class into groups that are working independently. The first time they teach a module, they will probably rely heavily on the teacher's guide and skip many of the optional activities. These behaviors indicate that teachers are still learning how to use the materials and have not yet assimilated them and made them their own. This level of expertise is often referred to as *mechanical use.*

It's essential that teachers new to inquiry have support at their schools throughout the school year. Particularly beneficial at this stage are opportunities for mentoring sessions with more experienced teachers.

Phase II: The Competent Stage
When teachers begin to feel comfortable with the materials and are ready to modify the lessons in a science module to reflect their

students' particular needs and interests, they are at the *competent stage*. It takes most teachers at least five years to reach this level of proficiency. At this stage, the professional development program takes on a different cast. Teachers are now interested in exploring in greater depth such topics as constructivist theory and the learning cycle, cooperative learning techniques, assessment strategies, and how to integrate science into other areas of the curriculum. Many teachers are also interested in learning more about the science content of the modules they are teaching. At this stage, the school should provide opportunities for small discussion groups for teachers engaged in teaching inquiry-centered science.

After being involved in these different professional development programs, teachers may begin to develop their own ideas for additional activities and extensions and look for other ways to modify the lessons. They may begin experimenting with different kinds of assessments and, if students are interested, with conducting a long-term class research project.

Phase III: The Expert Stage

The final phase in a teacher's professional development is the *expert stage*. If we could peek into a highly experienced teacher's science classroom, we would notice a few distinguishing features immediately. First, there is the sound of "organized noise" in the classroom. Children may be moving about, discussing ideas with classmates, and taking turns gathering materials at the distribution center. The teacher is moving around, too, listening to students' ideas, answering questions, and asking questions to help groups take the next step in completing an experiment or organizing results. By now, the teacher is not disturbed by the cup of water that spilled or the soil on the desktops. There is energy and excitement in the room.

Such teachers have become what is called "expert." They have reached this level through a combination of time, experience, their own enthusiasm, and effective professional development, both in the school and outside. According to the *National Science Education Standards*, "successful teachers are skilled observers of students, as well as knowledgeable about science and how it is learned. Teachers match their actions to the particular needs of the students, deciding when and how to guide—when to demand more rigorous grappling by the students, when to provide information, and when to connect students with other sources."[4]

The goal of professional development is to raise all teachers in a school district to the expert level. Doing so requires time, commitment, and energy on the part of both teachers and administrators. The next section explores a few strategies for professional development programs that have helped teachers grow professionally.

Strategies for Change

The professional development strategies listed below have been used in many school districts throughout the country. These strategies have been tested in a variety of settings and have proven to be effective in introducing large numbers of teachers to inquiry-centered science.

Lead Teachers

Many districts have initiated their professional development programs by beginning with a small group of teachers, called *lead teachers* or *mentor teachers,* who have demonstrated interest and expertise in inquiry-centered science teaching. This group is usually selected by administrators to represent each grade level in the district. Identifying and training this group of lead teachers is a key step in this professional development strategy.

Lead teachers can serve a variety of roles. In some districts, such as Montgomery County, Maryland, and the East Baton Rouge Parish Public School System in Louisiana, a cadre of lead teachers is responsible for conducting professional development activities for other teachers in the district. Those teachers also assist with materials support issues and are available to respond to questions that other teachers have about the program. Some hold workshops at faculty meetings. Others provide leadership at districtwide institutes. Lead teachers may often be called upon to field-test new modules, serve on curriculum selection committees, work with administrators to expand or modify selected modules, or develop new approaches to student assessment.

Although the lead-teacher strategy has been successful in many districts, some teachers and administrators have encountered obstacles in their efforts to implement it. For example, in Huntsville, Alabama, teachers liked being introduced to the modules by fellow teachers, but they did not want to view a fellow teacher as a supervisor. In addition, some administrators have been unable to provide lead teachers with the time to actually "lead." These teachers find themselves so busy with their own classroom responsibilities that they don't have time to work with other teachers. Without time to mentor other teachers, lead teachers can serve only a limited function.

Schools nationwide are encountering the problem of teachers not having time for professional development. Time will continue to be an issue in a climate of budget cutting, especially in communities where parents exert pressure on the system to limit the number of professional days for teachers. Administrators and lead teachers committed to this approach must be aware that they will be grappling with such issues as they strive to implement the science program.

Partnerships Between School Districts and Research Scientists

In the 1960s, scientists' involvement in professional development consisted largely of having scientists go into the classroom and take over the science class for a specified number of lessons. To no one's surprise, teachers felt intimidated by the scientists, and the scientists often didn't know how to present their subject so that it made sense to their young audiences.

To overcome these concerns while still taking advantage of scientists' expertise, many districts have developed innovative forms of teacher-scientist collaborations. For example, the Pasadena Unified School District Science Program (formerly known as Project SEED), a teacher-scientist partnership between the Pasadena Unified School District and the California Institute of Technology (CalTech), has perfected a strategy in which lead teachers work collaboratively with scientists to introduce teachers to science curriculum modules. Scientists also conduct sessions with lead teachers at institutes, where the scientists serve as content specialists or in an advisory role, suggesting ways to bring inquiry to the classroom. CalTech scientists also attend follow-up meetings with teachers, where they are available to answer questions teachers have after working with the modules. This collaborative approach has also been adopted by City Science, a partnership between the San Francisco Unified School District and the University of California at San Francisco.

Some districts, such as Montgomery County, Maryland, have provided the scientists with some training before they begin their work with elementary school teachers. In a preliminary meeting, scientists learn about the concerns of teachers and some pedagogical strategies. This training gives scientists important background knowledge about teachers, so it becomes easier for the scientists to provide appropriate support and knowledge.

Scientists at other institutions, such as science museums, can work with teachers in a similar way. For example, the Buffalo Museum of Science in New York has a partnership with the Buffalo School District, where scientists are involved in professional development activities and in establishing a centralized science materials support center. The Franklin Institute, in Philadelphia, played a key role in introducing Philadelphia's public schools to inquiry-centered science.

Partnerships with Business and Industry

Successful partnerships can develop between school districts and local industrial corporations. These corporations frequently have expertise that can be shared with teachers. Some corporate sponsors, such as Hewlett-Packard, have created on-line computer networks to answer teachers' questions about the particular topics their classes are investigating. Chapter 9 explores school partnerships with business and industry in more detail.

Some school districts incorporate combinations of these models into their professional development programs. For example, Montgomery County, Maryland, and Spokane, Washington, use the lead-teacher approach but also make use of university scientists for some portions of the professional development program. Alternatively, a corporate partnership may assist lead teachers by providing them with expertise in a particular subject area. In these ways, school districts can modify these strategies to fit their needs.

6

The Nuts and
Bolts of
Change

Key Points

Professional development is key to the success of the inquiry-centered science program. Creating an environment of collegiality and collaboration, providing teachers with the time to learn, and designing the program appropriately are among the strategies school districts have used to ensure that the professional development program is effective.

Progressive levels of professional development can be designed for teachers new to inquiry, for those at the intermediate stage, and for those who have reached the expert level.

Several strategies, including the lead-teacher strategy, partnerships between school districts and research scientists, and partnerships with business and industry, have been used successfully in school districts nationwide.

For Further Reading

Calwelti, G., ed. 1993. *Challenges and Achievements of American Education: 1993 Yearbook of the Association for Supervision and Curriculum Development.* Alexandria, Va.: Association for Supervision and Curriculum Development.

Jackson, R. B. 1973. *Something of Value: A Summary of Findings and Recommendations for Improving Elementary Science in Massachusetts.* Cambridge, Mass.: Commonwealth of Massachusetts.

Joyce, B., ed. 1990. *Changing School Culture Through Staff Development: 1990 Yearbook of the Association for Supervision and Curriculum Development.* Alexandria, Va.: Association for Supervision and Curriculum Development.

National Research Council. 1996. *National Science Education Standards.* Washington, D.C.: National Academy Press.

National Research Council. 1996. *The Role of Scientists in the Professional Development of Teachers.* Washington, D.C.: National Academy Press.

Raizen, S. A., and A. M. Michelsohn, eds. 1994. *The Future of Science in Elementary Schools: Educating Prospective Teachers.* San Francisco: Jossey-Bass.

Sigma Xi. 1994. *Scientists, Educators, and National Standards: Action at the Local Level.* Research Triangle Park, N.C.: Sigma Xi.

Whitla, D. K., and D. C. Pinck. 1973. *Essentially Elementary Science: A Report on the Status of Elementary Science in Massachusetts Schools.* Cambridge, Mass.: Office of Instructional Research and Evaluation, in the Harvard Faculty of Arts and Sciences, and Harvard Graduate School of Education.

W. K. Kellogg Foundation. 1993. *How to Unravel Science Mysteries for Young Minds Without Unraveling: A Summary of Lessons Learned.* Battle Creek, Mich.: W. K. Kellogg Foundation.

Establishing a
Science Materials
Support Center

If you want to encourage elementary school teachers to teach science through inquiry, you have to provide them with the right stuff at the right time. You have to give teachers a deal they can't refuse.

— Larry Small, "Science Materials Support," 1992

To teach inquiry-centered science modules, the teacher needs all the "stuff" of science—containers, scales, chemicals, and living organisms. These materials make science inviting to children and bring them into the world of scientists and how they work.

In the past, teachers often had the responsibility of gathering the materials outlined in the teacher's guide to teach inquiry-centered science. This did not prove to be realistic or efficient, because few elementary teachers had the time or the expertise to do this job well. Experience has shown that science will be taught more effectively if science materials are managed by the school district and made available to teachers when they need them. The most effective way for a school district to do this is to create a science materials support center.

The purpose of such a center is to provide all the materials teachers need to teach inquiry-centered science modules in "ready-to-use" condition. Although the idea is simple, implementing it is not. The manager of a materials support center must consider myriad details to ensure that elementary science teachers receive what they need when they need it. Issues that must be considered include how to manage large quantities of materials, replenish kits that have been depleted of consumable supplies, keep the inventory of hundreds of items up to date, order new supplies from the most economical sources, and ensure that the kits arrive in the classroom on schedule.

Although there are other ways to support teachers with science materials, the most efficient and cost-effective approach is to establish a central science materials center that is operated by the school district. Many school districts engaged in reform have discovered the importance of this critical element. George Hein, consultant for the National Science Resources Center's Elementary Science Leadership Institute program, and Carol Baldassari and Laura Hudson found that most districts that sent teams to the Leadership Institutes between 1989 and 1995 recognized the importance of establishing a materials support center and are taking steps to ensure that this element is in place.[1]

Larry Small, the former science coordinator of School District 54 in Schaumburg, Illinois, founded one of the first successful central materials support centers. He recounts from his own experience why a central materials center is so effective:

> In the early development of our system, the materials were purchased by central warehouse personnel and sent to the individual schools for storage in the school's science "closet." The audiovisual materials were housed in each school's library or resource center. Some science units were contained in one box. Other units used baking soda, vinegar, soda straws, and other common grocery store items. These items were purchased and stocked on the shelf of each school's science closet. About midway through the first year of the new program, the boxed unit had been used by one or two teach-

ers. Once the consumables had been used up, the science unit did not get taught. The units that needed materials not contained in this box but on the closet shelf had an even worse record of use. These units were never taught at all.[2]

A central materials support center can solve most of the problems that Small describes. Through central coordination across the district, important tasks such as purchasing materials, keeping track of inventory, sorting and packaging items, assembling kits, distributing kits to classrooms, and refurbishing them for reuse can be accomplished efficiently.

Because there are so many benefits to this approach, the emphasis of this chapter will be on describing how to set up a science materials support center for a school district. The discussion begins with issues that need to be considered in planning a materials support center and then focuses on expenses associated with starting and maintaining the materials support center.

Some school districts, such as those that are very small or that cannot afford to set up a centralized system or those that are managed by a site-based approach, may wish to consider other ways to provide teachers with the science materials they need. Therefore, the chapter concludes with a description of alternative types of science materials support systems.

Planning a Science Materials Support Center

The establishment of a systemwide science materials center should be one element of the district's overall strategic plan. Plans for setting up the materials center must begin early in the program, when the first curriculum modules are being selected. As in all aspects of establishing the science program, it makes sense to start small, circulating only a few modules to a few schools. If procedures are established on a small scale, the materials center will be better prepared to expand to handle more modules and more schools. Because of the complexity of the tasks and procedures involved, establishing an efficient materials center will take between three and five years. Maintaining the center will be an ongoing effort.

The issues that need to be addressed are practical. For example, where is the materials center going to be housed? How much

Workers pack science kits at the science materials support center in Montgomery County, Maryland.

space will be needed? Who will staff the facility? Is there money in the budget for a separate staff, or will current staff members, such as the science coordinator and his or her administrative assistant, have to assume additional responsibilities? These issues are explored in more detail below.

Space

For a large school district, processing science kits requires a large space, such as a warehouse or an unused school building. A single room in a school building or the corner of a districtwide resource center will not be sufficient. Small school districts, on the other hand, may find that one or two rooms in a school building are sufficient. Ideally, the materials center will be in a large space close to an outside entrance that can be used for receiving shipments of materials and for moving science kits in and out of the building.

Despite careful planning, space has proven to be a problem in many school districts. For example, Montgomery County Public Schools, in Maryland, moved its center three times before the district found the right space. Spokane District 81 in Spokane, Washington, encountered another kind of problem related to space. The warehouse designated to store kits had formerly been used to store textbooks. Much to the dismay of science program coordinators, there was not enough room in the warehouse for the science kits because the textbooks hadn't been removed in time. Program designers must anticipate the possibility of road-blocks such as these, which can cause major setbacks in program implementation.

Management

In many school districts, responsibility for the science program is shared by many players. For example, one office may be responsible for scheduling kit deliveries, while another office is in charge of day-to-day operations. To establish a well-functioning center, these offices must be able to communicate and solve problems together.

Staffing

Most materials support centers begin with a small staff—perhaps a manager and one full-time staff member or a few part-time employees. Identifying a strong manager is crucial, because that person must oversee operations: ensuring that the inventory is being kept up-to-date, that the kits are ready to go out on time, and that pickup and delivery take place according to schedule.

As more teachers begin using inquiry-centered science modules, additional part-time employees may be necessary. Some large school districts, which may package as many as 3,000 science kits a year, have called on high school students and senior citizens to work during peak processing seasons. Both of these strategies have worked well.

Inventory

Keeping track of the inventory and updating materials lists for the science kits is part of the work of the materials center. The more specific the lists, the better. Detailed lists help staff become aware of what they have in stock, what items are being depleted, and what they need to reorder. Most school districts have established formal procedures to ensure that supplies are reordered and received before they are needed.

Packaging
Preparing the kits for delivery is highly labor-intensive. At designated times of the year, staff needs to be available to prepare the kits for the teachers. Some districts may decide to manufacture the kits themselves; others focus on refurbishing science kits that have been purchased from commercial suppliers. In either case, the school district must be aware of its needs and plan ways to meet them well in advance.

Scheduling
The schedule serves two functions: It specifies the date for the delivery and pickup of science kits for teachers and the time the kits will be at the center for refurbishing. Districts have developed different scheduling strategies. One strategy that has been used effectively is placing science kits on a nine-week schedule and sending them out according to subject area. This means that schools participating in the program receive all the life and earth science kits at about the same time and must be ready to return them at the end of nine weeks. During the nine weeks that the life and earth science kits are in the schools, the materials support center can refurbish the physical science kits so that they are ready to go out at the beginning of the next nine-week cycle. Teachers are responsible for preparing the kits for pickup and knowing where the designated pickup point is.

Delivery
The plan must cover how the kits will be transported from the science materials center to the schools. Some districts use the services established for delivering multimedia materials and other supplies to schools for the science kits. Other materials centers have created their own delivery systems. Each district needs to consider which option best suits its needs.

Service
All teachers must feel confident that their materials will be ready when they need them. When teachers need additional materials or encounter unanticipated problems, they need to be confident that someone at the district level is responsible for supporting them. In addition, teachers with materials problems need to be able to ask lead teachers in their school to help them.

Need for Special Handling Procedures

It is important that the materials support center have a plan for receiving and maintaining the animals and plants used in the modules. The materials center should also assist teachers by developing guidelines for maintaining living organisms in the classroom.

Safety

Staff at the materials center should be aware of basic safety precautions, such as providing goggles for students who will be working with chemicals, even common ones such as salt and baking soda, and not using seeds that have been treated with fungicides or pesticides. Guidelines on recommended safety precautions should also be provided to teachers.

Cost-Saving Measures

Multiple Uses of Kits

In planning the materials support center, school administrators must prepare realistic, cost-effective budgets. Operating a materials support center does cost money. Districts must be prepared to invest in the science materials for the kits, but once they make that commitment, they can save money by using each kit several times each year and relying on cost-saving measures when purchasing consumable materials.

To understand why using a kit at least twice during the school year keeps costs down, consider the following example. Let's assume that a kit costs $400. If 30 students, or one class, use that kit, the cost per student is $13.33. If you take that same $400 kit and spend $100 to refurbish it, the total cost of the kit increases to $500, but two classes, or 60 students, can use it. This means that the cost of the kit per student decreases from $13.33 to $8.33. And if the kit is used three times, refurbishment costs $200, but because 90 students can use it, per capita costs drop to $6.66.

Refurbishing Costs

Many factors contribute to refurbishing costs. In figuring out these expenses, the materials support center staff needs to consider personnel costs, costs for consumable items such as chemicals and batteries, and costs for lost or broken nonconsumable materials, such as graduated cylinders and hand lenses. The two biggest operating expenses for a materials support center are staff and replacing consumable and nonconsumable items.

To keep personnel costs down, many programs have a bare-bones staff and rely on volunteers for additional help. Over time, however, as the program grows and more kits are circulating throughout the system, more staff will be necessary.

There are many ways for the materials center to save money in replacing both consumable and nonconsumable items. Staff can purchase raw materials directly from manufacturers or whole-sale distributors. Although such materials must be bought in bulk, purchasing items in this way leads to tremendous cost savings. Working with more than one supplier for each item or kit and ne-gotiating the best price through a bid process can also save large amounts of money. Through the bid process, districts may find local suppliers who can provide better service at a lower price than national outlets. Some materials centers have discovered that a local hardware or garden supply store can supply certain items, such as potting soil and aquarium gravel, through special orders. Local stores may also offer free delivery.

Finally, staff at science materials centers can be creative in their search for inexpensive materials. In addition to local tele-phone directories, many centers have found it useful to consult *The Thomas Register of American Manufacturers,* a multivolume set of books that contains more than 50,000 product and service head-ings. This register may be available at the school district purchas-ing office.

Other Types of Materials Centers

Although experience has revealed that for the average school dis-trict, establishing a districtwide science materials center is the most effective way to supply materials, there are other options. The list that follows identifies some alternate strategies that have been used to supply materials to inquiry-centered science programs. These approaches may be especially suitable for small districts that can't afford to establish their own centralized system or for dis-tricts that have adopted a site-based management system.

Consortium-Based System

A consortium of school districts may decide to operate a science materials center as a cooperative venture. Consortium programs generally charge participating districts a fee based on the number of teachers and schools that will be served. For example, the center in Huntsville, Alabama, charges participating school districts a flat fee of $300 per teacher per year, as well as an additional fee (about $6) per student for refurbishing. Other consortia, such as the Einstein Project, in Green Bay, Wisconsin, charge a $100 rental fee each time a kit is used. Consortia have the advantage of quantity purchasing discounts. Small districts may find the consortium approach useful, especially if a neighboring district has already established a materials center.

Site-Based System

This is a system in which all of the materials needed to teach science at all grade levels are stored in one designated location within in a school building. Storage space may be set aside in the school's resource center or a storeroom. A few schools have fully equipped science labs where teachers can hold their science classes. Site-based organization has the advantage of ensuring that materials are accessible to teachers throughout the school year. However, problems can occur if maintaining the materials is seen as a teacher's responsibility. If only one kit is provided for each grade level, teachers must share the kit and someone must accept responsibility for refurbishing it. Scheduling the use of the materials and ordering replacement items can become burdensome.

Classroom-Based System

In this system, each classroom has all the supplies and print materials needed for the curriculum. Such a system allows teachers flexibility in scheduling when the science units will be taught throughout the year, because all the materials are always at hand. This approach also has major disadvantages. Teachers may have trouble finding space in their classrooms to store the kits. They may not have the time to keep careful inventory records so that sufficient supplies can be maintained, or they may not realize the importance of reordering supplies in a timely fashion. Finally, there is a

danger that the expense of maintaining materials will fall to the individual teachers committed to teaching by inquiry. In the past, these problems often resulted in the abandonment of inquiry-centered science programs.

Where to Go for Information

For more information about how to establish a materials center, your district may want to contact the Association of Science Materials Centers (ASMC), c/o Science and Social Sciences Resource Specialist, Mesa Public Schools, 143 South Alma School Road, Mesa, AZ 85120-1096, or call (602) 898-7815. ASMC members meet annually to share information about the design of science teaching apparatus, sources of supply, and strategies for reducing the cost of inquiry-centered science instruction.

Key Points

▶ Issues to consider in planning a materials support center include space, personnel, inventory systems, delivery, refurbishing, and cost.

▶ The most efficient way to supply materials to schools is through a districtwide science materials center. This approach minimizes costs and ensures that materials needed to teach science arrive in the classroom on time, in a "ready-to-use" condition.

▶ In some cases, other approaches may be useful. The consortium approach may be particularly helpful for small districts, while the site-based and classroom systems may be the only options in districts where there is no financial or political support for establishing a science materials center. However, there is no evidence that these systems can be successfully maintained over time.

For Further Reading

Harlen, W. 1989. *Developing Science in the Primary Classroom.* Portsmouth, N.H.: Heinemann Educational Books, Inc.

Lapp, D. M. 1980. "The Need for Teacher Support Systems." *The National Elementary Principal* January 61-66.

Loucks-Horsley, S., R. Kapitan, M. D. Carlson, P. J. Kuerbis, R. C. Clark, G. M. Melle, T. P. Sachse, and E. Walton. 1990. *Elementary School Science for the '90s.* Andover, Mass.: The NETWORK, Inc., and Alexandria, Va.: Association for Supervision and Curriculum Development.

Small, L. 1992. "Science Materials Support," unpublished white paper by former science supervisor for Schaumburg, Ill.

The Thomas Register of American Manufacturers. New York: Thomas Publishing Company.

8

Assessment Strategies for Inquiry-Centered Science

Assessing science through paper-and-pencil tests is akin to assessing a basketball player's skills by giving a written test. We may find out what someone knows about basketball, but we won't know how well that person plays the game.

— **George Hein and Sabra Price,**
Active Assessments for Active Science, **1994**

Principals and science coordinators often hear teachers lament that traditional assessments simply don't work in inquiry-centered classrooms. "Paper-and-pencil tests only give information on part of what we teach," they say. "We need something else to use to give us a better picture of what our students know and are able to do."

Traditional tests—usually multiple-choice, short-answer tests given at the end of a unit of study—cannot assess all the richness of learning that takes place in the inquiry-centered science classroom. A multiple-choice test cannot effectively evaluate whether students have learned how to design an experiment, make accurate observations and measurements, analyze data, and reach reasonable conclusions. Multiple-choice tests are also not very effective in assessing student understanding of concepts such as buoyancy or the role bees play in the life cycle of plants. Measuring students' grasp of these skills and concepts requires alternative forms of assessment.

This chapter outlines several ways to structure assessment activities that can effectively determine each student's progress toward the attainment of science inquiry skills and concepts. To illustrate each form of assessment, we have included examples from three curriculum programs—Full Option Science System (FOSS), Insights, and Science and Technology for Children (STC). Throughout the chapter, we will concentrate on how the teacher can assess student learning on a daily basis.

The chapter also describes strategies that can be used to assess the science program as a whole. We present guidelines school districts can use to determine how the implementation of the science program is proceeding.

Assessing Student Learning

Just as it is challenging to institute inquiry-based instruction in the classroom, so is it difficult to incorporate new assessment strategies into classroom evaluation. For this reason, it is reassuring to know that teachers need not create new assessment strategies on their own. Many of the national curriculum programs include such strategies in their teacher's guides. These suggestions provide a good starting point.

Most teachers find it helpful to begin to use the new assessment strategies slowly and carefully. It is neither necessary nor advisable to eliminate traditional testing. In fact, one of the guiding principles behind assessment is that the more diverse the strategies used, the more the teacher can learn about each student. Over time, each teacher will discover ways to balance traditional tests and alternative assessments to obtain a complete picture of how well students are progressing.

Although the focus in this section is on assessment in the classroom, it is important to recognize that assessment is a contro-

During an informal assessment for a module on ecosystems, a teacher talks with fifth-grade students about their observations.

versial issue in science education. Within the classroom, using a range of assessment tools provides information on both student learning and future teaching strategies. Within a school district, however, standardized tests are often used as a means of making schools accountable for student learning.

Our focus here is on helping teachers develop more effective strategies for assessing student learning in their classrooms. The following assessment strategies have been used effectively in many inquiry-centered science classrooms throughout the country. Many of them have been incorporated into national science curriculum programs.

Matched Pre- and Post-Module Assessments

Pre- and post-module assessments serve two important functions. The first is to track how much students have learned during the unit. For example, the teacher could ask a question or assign an investigation at the beginning of each module to find out how much students know about the subject. At the end of the module, students could answer the same question or perform the same investigation, enabling the teacher to observe how their understanding of a subject has grown.

Such assessments can take many forms. For example, many modules in the STC elementary science curriculum begin with a brainstorming session during which children are asked what they know about a subject and what they would like to learn about it. At the end of the module, they are asked the same questions again, giving the teacher an opportunity to assess how much students have learned over the course of the unit.

A pre-module assessment can also give the teacher information on what questions students are interested in pursuing. As the class progresses through the unit, the teacher can refer to the pre-module assessment to further refine teaching strategies. The post-module data can then be used as a way for the teacher to measure the success of his or her teaching strategies.

Other examples of pre- and post-module assessments include having students write about a subject, draw a picture, or perform a simple experiment. These devices give teachers important "before-and-after" information. Figure 8-1 shows examples of pre- and post-module assessments.

The Insights elementary science program has a more formal pre-module assessment. Each module in this program begins with an introductory questionnaire that is linked to the goals of that module. The questionnaire may include content-related questions as well as questions designed to assess students' problem-solving abilities. At the end of the module, students complete the questionnaire again; the two versions of the questionnaire provide teachers with a written record of students' progress. Younger students complete the questionnaire through interviews. Figure 8-2 shows part of an introductory questionnaire from the Insights *Reading the Environment* module.

Embedded Assessments
These assessments are woven, or embedded, into the instructional sequence in the module. They may be part of the activities that naturally occur in a lesson or a logical extension of the lesson's

Weiss, Brandon

What I know about paper 1. its made of trees 2. it has fibers and its used in a lot of things

WHAT I LEARNED ABOUT PAPER ✓
WEISS, BRANDON
LS. 17

I KNOW THAT ALL PAPER HAS FIBERS.

I KNOW THAT ALL PAPER HAS A DIFFERENT OPACITY.

I KNOW THAT ALL PAPER HAS A DIFFERENT TEAR FACTOR.

I KNOW THAT ALL OLDER PAPER USED TO BE ME OF CLOTH AND EVEN MUMMIE RAPPINGS. SOME WORKERS GOT SICK BECAUSE THE RAPPINGS WERE NOT CLEAN AT ALL.

ALL PAPER GOES THOUGH MANY PROCESSES TO BECOME PAPER. CARDBOARD GOES THROUGH THE SAME PROCESSES AS

Brandon Weiss
Grade 6

SOME E PAPER.

THE ART OF PAPER BEGAN WITH THE CHINESE.

THE PAPER WE ARE MAKING IS MADE BY SHREDDING AND TEARING THE PAPER YOU ARE RECYCLING. WHEN YOU ARE FINISHED WITH SHREDDING AND TEARING MIX THE TORN PAPER WITH WATER. PUT THE MIXTURE IN A BUCKET MIX WITH AN EGG BEATER UNTIL LOOKS LIKE PULP. POOR INTO MOLD AND THE DECAL.

THEN DRAIN OUT THERE WILL STILL BE SOME WATER LEFT IN THE THE PAPER, LAY THE PAPER DOWN SOMEWHERE AND LET IT DRY OVERNIGHT.

I KNOW HOW TO EMBED AND EMBOSS.

Figure 8-1. Pre- and post-module writing samples and drawings from the sixth-grade module The Technology of Paper *(STC) and the second-grade module* The Life Cycle of Butterflies *(STC)*

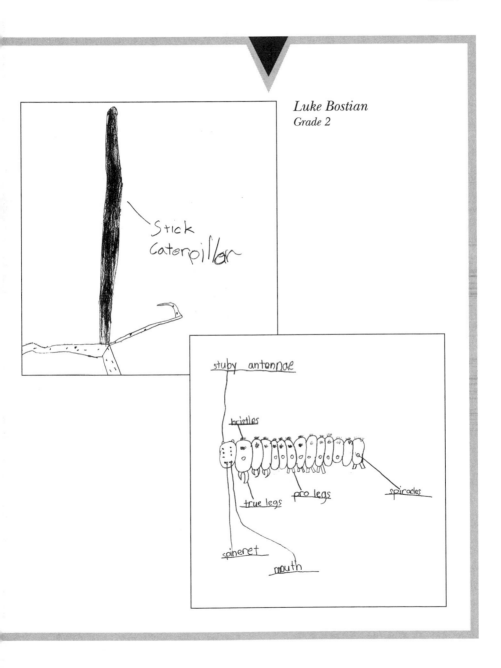

Luke Bostian
Grade 2

Stick
Caterpillar

stuby antennae

bristles

true legs

pro legs

spiracles

spineret

mouth

Name _____ Date _____

Reading the Environment
Introductory Questionnaire

DIRECTIONS TO STUDENTS

Answer each question below as completely as possible in the space provided. Use the back of the paper or an extra sheet if you need more space. In some of the questions, there are words in italics. If you think you know the meaning of the word (even if you are not sure), try to answer the question. If you do not know the meaning of the word at all, and cannot even guess, write: "I do not know this word." If there are any other words (not in italics) whose meaning you do not know, ask your teacher to explain them.

1. Think of something in your neighborhood that is not living and that has changed in the past couple of years. In the space below, name it and describe as completely as you can what it was like in the past, before it changed.

*Figure 8-2. Introductory questionnaire from the fourth-grade
module* Reading the Environment *(Insights)*

2. What evidence do you see that tells you the thing you named in question 1 has changed?

Describe below what this thing is like now. State exactly what the change is that you have noticed. For example: "There was a change in the street. It has cracks in it. The evidence I see is a crack and the street around it is breaking into small pieces. I think it is being worn down."

3. What do you think caused the change(s) you noted in question 2?

4. Give an example of a *fossil* and describe what it looks like.

EDC © 1991

central activity. Embedded assessments are based on the assumption that assessment and learning are two sides of the same coin. In fact, many educators assert that from the students' vantage point, there should be a seamless flow between instruction and assessment.[1] The biggest difference between an embedded assessment and other learning activities is that the assessment is designed to enable the teacher to obtain and record information about student learning.

The following are examples of embedded assessments:

▶ After studying STC's *Electric Circuits* module for fourth-graders, students are asked to wire a cardboard house. The activity enables the teacher to assess whether students can apply what they have learned about circuits to a "real-life" situation.

▶ Throughout the FOSS *Paper* module (a kindergarten unit), students are invited to engage in discussions that reveal their understanding of key concepts.

▶ At the end of STC's fifth-grade *Food Chemistry* module, students use tests they learned about in the unit to determine which nutrients are in a marshmallow.

Prediction Activities
A prediction is different from a guess because it is based on previous experience and knowledge of a subject. By asking students to make predictions at appropriate times, teachers can assess the science concepts their students have mastered and how well they can apply that knowledge to a new situation. For example, during a module on buoyancy (STC's *Floating and Sinking*), students may be given an assortment of objects and asked to predict which ones will float and which will sink. If students consider both weight and volume in making their predictions, the teacher will know that students have gained some understanding of the concept. If they guess randomly, they are telling the teacher that they have a limited understanding of the concept. In either case, the teacher has gained valuable information.

Final Assessments

These assessments are used at the end of a science unit or module. Although many final assessments include paper-and-pencil tests, they can take many other forms. Examples of final assessments are described below.

Hands-on Assessments. This type of assessment provides an opportunity for teachers to observe how well students can perform an experiment similar to one they worked on during the module. Hands-on assessments allow teachers to see how students approach a problem, gather data, record results, and draw conclusions from their findings. For example, after experimenting with water in the FOSS *Water* module, students are given a new problem that must be solved through experimentation. The Insights module *Reading the Environment* has a hands-on assessment in which students are asked to design an experiment that will help them decide what kind of stone to use for building in a city where acid rain is a problem.

Another way to organize hands-on assessments is for the teacher to set up stations throughout the room that offer a series of tasks for children to complete. For example, after finishing a module on chemical tests, students may be asked to perform a filtration task at one table, a mixing task at another, and data analysis at a third table. By observing how the students go about the tasks, reviewing the kinds of records they make, and checking their results, the teacher will gain information about what the students have learned. This work can be done individually or in cooperative groups.

Paper-and-Pencil Tests. These are questions included at the end of the unit. The FOSS curriculum divides paper-and-pencil assessments into two categories: pictorial assessments and reflective questions assessments. FOSS pictorial assessments evaluate how well students can think through problems that require both knowledge and the application of ideas to a new situation. For example, pictorial assessments from the *Water* module include figuring out why a plastic bottle of water left in the car trunk overnight cracked when the temperature dropped and why water that spilled on the sidewalk seemed to disappear.

Reflective assessments evaluate how well students can express themselves in writing, as indicated by the way students respond to problem-solving questions.

In the STC module *Measuring Time*, students are asked to graph hypothetical data, analyze data from a graph, and discuss in detail reasons for the moon's phases. Activities such as these encourage students to go beyond simply recalling isolated pieces of information and to think critically in applying knowledge to new situations.

Science Notebooks. Students can be asked to prepare individual science notebooks that include all the observations and records generated during the module. The notebooks may include stories and poems (see Figure 8-3), record sheets, charts, tables, and graphs. Drawings also reveal what students have learned (see Figure 8-4). The teacher should assess the level of detail, use of labels, and quality of explanations accompanying the drawings.

Science notebooks are useful for both teachers and students. Notebooks are a powerful assessment tool for teachers and an effective way for students to keep a record of what they have done in the module.

A portfolio is a selected group of student work. Students themselves can select pieces that they feel represent significant learning. Usually, the teacher and students work together to develop selection criteria, which may include materials that were the hardest to do or projects that provoked the most learning. Through this process, students have an opportunity to reflect on what they've learned.

Informal Assessments

Many teachers also find it helpful to conduct informal assessments of students' progress. These involve reviewing written materials, observing students at work, and simply walking around the room and listening to students' conversations. By asking the right questions, teachers can uncover students' reasoning and the steps they used to solve problems. The questions that students ask can also be a source of information about their understanding. In addition, individual and group presentations can give teachers insights into students' interpretation of what they have learned. Finally, questions posed by students following presentations can provide opportunities to gather important information.

Faith Washington
Grade 2

Yesterday I put clay in a
funnel and some of the water
came through. Some of the
water was orange. At first
I thought it would't come
though. But it did.

Daniel Hall
Grade 2

What is soil? ☺ *Very good!*

Soil is made of sand and
lots of minerals. It needs
water to help plants grow. It
grows food for us. Soil is clay.
Soil helps the environment.
Soil helps grow flowers and vegetables.
We need soil to grow plants.

rd Sheet 7-E   Name: Daniel Hall

Date: 5/5/94

Settling

Draw what you see
just after shaking.

t does this tell you about the mystery mixture?

u can see clay and sand
mixed in the magnafying
glass. It looks like clay after
its shaken.

Lunden Letofsky
Grade 2

Figure 8-3. Writing samples from the second-grade module Soils *(STC)*

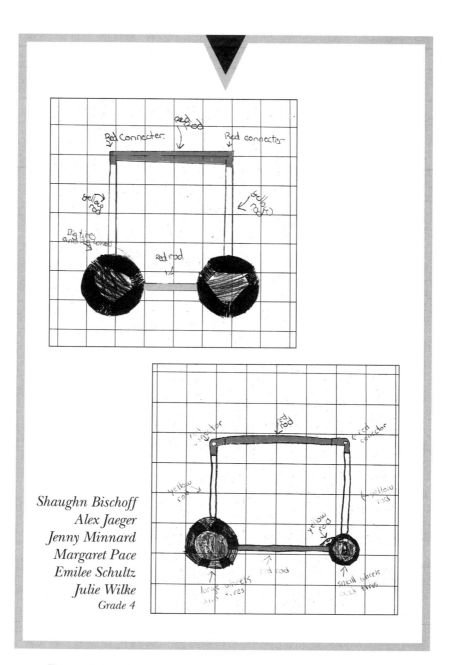

Shaughn Bischoff
Alex Jaeger
Jenny Minnard
Margaret Pace
Emilee Schultz
Julie Wilke
Grade 4

Figure 8-4. Student drawings from the fourth-grade module
Motion and Design *(STC)*

Documentation and Record Keeping

One of the hardest parts of incorporating alternative assessments into the inquiry-centered science program is developing an accurate record-keeping system. Many teacher's guides include record-keeping charts that help teachers focus on the goals of each assessment instrument.

For example, the STC program includes an observation sheet that teachers may photocopy and use in evaluating each student. The sheet highlights each module's key concepts and skills. For one module, *Balancing and Weighing,* concepts listed include the relationship between the amount of weight and its position on the balance beam, what is meant by the term "weighing," and the relationship between weight and volume. Skills listed include performing simple experiments with a balance beam, using an equal-arm balance, and applying strategies for comparing and weighing to solve problems. Alongside each of these concepts and skills is a space for the teacher to write observations. Figure 8-5 is a sample recording chart from the STC program. The chief advantages of this chart are that it provides a structure for teachers to use as they experiment with new assessment strategies and it can be adapted to suit the needs and record-keeping styles of different teachers.

The FOSS program includes a student worksheet with each of its assessments. To help teachers interpret the results on these sheets, the teacher's guide includes a chart that identifies the purpose of each question. For example, teachers are told that the purpose of the question about the cracked water bottle is to give students an opportunity to explain what happens when water freezes. The purpose of the question about the water that disappeared is to determine whether the students can explain how water evaporates. Figure 8-6 shows a sample observation chart from FOSS's *Water* module.

The Insights program has four parts to its assessment framework: the introductory questionnaire (pre-assessment), the embedded assessment, the post-module assessment, and ongoing assessments throughout the module. The teacher uses student profile charts to record the ongoing assessments and an evaluation rubric to inform the analysis of the formal pieces. The rubric ranges from "0" (no answer or "I don't know") to "5" (a complete and correct response). Figure 8-7 shows the complete Insights rubric.

Blackline Master

Balancing and Weighing: **Observations of Student Performance**

STUDENT'S NAME:

Concepts	Observations
• Balance is affected by the amount of weight, the position of weight, and the position of the fulcrum.	
• Weighing is the process of balancing an object against a certain number of standard units.	
• The weight of an object is not determined by its size.	
• Equal volumes of different foods will not all have equal weights; equal weights of different foods will not all have equal volumes.	

Skills

• Performing simple experiments with balance.

• Applying previous experiences with balancing to build mobiles.

• Using an equal-arm balance to compare and weigh.

• Predicting the serial order for the weights of objects and foods.

• Applying strategies for comparing and weighing to solve problems.

• Recording results on record sheets, bar graphs, line plots, data tables, and Venn diagrams.

• Communicating ideas, observations, and experiences through writing, drawing, and discussion.

• Reading to learn more about balancing and weighing.

STC / *Balancing and Weighing*

Figure 8-5. Teacher's observation chart from the second-grade module Balancing and Weighing *(STC)*

Water Assessment

The Reflective Questions Assessment

The **Reflective Questions Assessment** is made up of written questions that ask students to describe and explain events. It takes students about 20 minutes to complete all the questions.

Getting Ready for the Reflective Questions Assessment

Make copies of the two student sheets for this assessment. The entire set of questions can be given at one sitting. The tasks can be easily completed by students at their own desks. No equipment is needed.

Doing the Reflective Questions Assessment

Instruct students to read each task carefully, then do what the directions say. In most cases they will be asked to explain events.

Recording the Results of the Reflective Questions Assessment

The answer sheet gives answers or reasonable responses to the tasks. Feel free to adjust the ranges for acceptable answers based on the capabilities of your students.

On the *Water Module Reflective Questions Assessment Teacher's Chart*, each task in the assessment is clearly delineated along the top margin. This sheet provides a convenient visual summary of individual students' and the class's understanding of water properties and interactions.

The simplest way to use the teacher's chart is to place a check beside each student's name under the appropriate task. A blank indicates that the student did not complete the task satisfactorily.

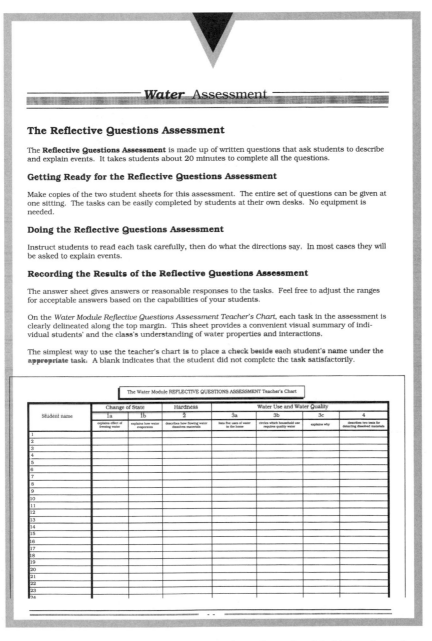

The Water Module REFLECTIVE QUESTIONS ASSESSMENT Teacher's Chart

Student name	Change of State		Hardness	Water Use and Water Quality			
	1a	1b	2	3a	3b	3c	4
	explains effect of freezing water	explains how water evaporates	describes how flowing water dissolves materials	lists five uses of water in the home	circles which household use requires quality water	explains why	describes two tests for detecting dissolved materials
1							
2							
3							
4							
5							
6							
7							
8							
9							
10							
11							
12							
13							
14							
15							
16							
17							
18							
19							
20							
21							
22							
23							
24							

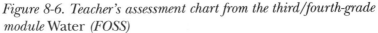

Figure 8-6. Teacher's assessment chart from the third/fourth-grade module Water *(FOSS)*

8

The Nuts and
Bolts of
Change

Introductory Questionnaire

Materials

For each student:
• Introductory Questionnaire
• extra paper if desired

> **NOTE**
>
> With the exception of words identified in italics, this is an assessment of understanding and experience, not an assessment of technical vocabulary. Note which students are having trouble with the language of the questionnaire. They may need extra help throughout the module.

Advance Preparation

• Make copies of the Introductory Questionnaire for each student.

• The questionnaire is intended as a written assessment; however, if you have students with special needs or limited English facility, you are encouraged to translate, paraphrase, or replace it with an interview .

• Familiarize yourself with the questions so as to be able to elaborate on them if students have trouble with particular words.

Evaluating the Introductory Questionnaire

Guidelines to code the level or depth of knowledge the student has about a concept or skill.

5 – a complete and correct response.

4 – an essentially correct response but one that omits some detail(s), or underlying explanations, or contains a slight inaccuracy.

3 – a response that is wrong or skimpy simply because the student does not know the concept or information.

2 – a naive conception: a response that is logical and coherent, and explains the data from the student's point of view, but happens to be scientifically wrong. There are many examples in history, such as the flat-earth theory. Note that this is different from an error that is made through mere lack of information.

1 – a naive, childish answer, or one that repeats the question.

0 – no answer, or "I don't know."

Figure 8-7. Rubric for evaluating the introductory questionnaire in an Insights module

Assessing the Science Program

In addition to assessing individual student progress with the new curriculum, school districts need two different kinds of information to assess the overall success of the science program. The first, and by far the most challenging to acquire, is information about whether the science program is resulting in significant changes in teaching and in student learning. The National Science Education Standards address this issue and acknowledge the difficulty in gathering this information, which needs to include the assessment of student knowledge and skills over time as well as changes in students' attitudes toward science. The second kind of information that school districts need is a measure of how they are progressing in their efforts to address each of the five elements of science education reform: curriculum, professional development, materials support, assessment, and administrative and community support.

George Hein, director of the Program Evaluation and Research Group at Lesley College in Cambridge, Massachusetts, and evaluator of the National Science Resources Center's (NSRC) Elementary Science Leadership Institute program, developed five rubrics that districts can use to assess the progress of their science programs (Figure 8-8). Each rubric corresponds to one of the elements of an effective elementary science program. The rubrics begin at level 0 (no action has been taken) and end at level 5 (complete implementation). Levels 2 through 4 describe the sequence typically followed in establishing a science program: developing a plan, initiating a small-scale reform effort, and expanding this effort each year.

Hein, Carol Baldassari, and Laura Hudson used the rubrics to determine the progress that school district teams that have attended the NSRC Leadership Institutes have made and to find out the paths they followed during their reform efforts. By interviewing each team and applying the rubrics to the responses, Hein and his colleagues determined that assessment has been the most difficult element to implement. Curriculum development and professional development have been easier to incorporate and have usually been done first. Establishing a materials support system has been accomplished as funding and administrative support have permitted.

Five Rubrics Used to Assess the Progress of Science Programs

Levels of Curriculum Reform

Level 0 Totally textbook-dominated program, no materials.

Level 1 Some (any) inquiry-centered science curriculum units based on individual school (or teacher) decision.

Level 2 District piloting inquiry-centered science curriculum units in part of system, with textbooks still dominant.

Level 3 Districtwide plan exists to introduce inquiry-centered science curriculum into entire system and/or early stage of implementation.

Level 4 Considerable progress in implementing inquiry-centered science curriculum units in entire system and/or evidence that texts are no longer used or are used primarily as supplements.

Level 5 Systemwide implementation of inquiry-centered elementary science program.

Levels of Professional Development Activities

Level 0 No teacher professional development program.

Level 1 Professional development program limited to introduction of hands-on science curriculum units to some teachers.

Level 2 A plan for professional development for all teachers and/or beginning of development of teacher leaders exists. Evidence of other activities (workshops, museum, college connections).

Level 3 Implementation of first-level workshops for most or all teachers in the district. A plan for advanced professional development activities for teacher leaders exists. Ongoing classroom support for up to one-half of teachers in district.

Level 4 Implementation of first-level activities for all teachers and provision for advanced professional development for all teachers. Evidence of systematic connection between district activities and opportunities at other institutions (museums, colleges, etc.). Ongoing classroom support for most teachers.

Level 5 Funded, coherent, continuous system for staff development articulated with developmental needs of all teachers, curriculum implementation, assessment, and other professional development activities.

Figure 8-8

Levels of Development of Centralized Materials Support Systems

Level 0 No plans for a materials support system.

Level 1 Recognized need for a materials support system for science, chose school-based or individual teacher responsibility, or began planning for center, but plans aborted.

Level 2 Temporary system that includes ordering and refurbishing materials and supplies for pilot classrooms or schools, or in the planning stage for districtwide system.

Level 3 Beginning to implement systemwide materials support system, but current system only partial: insufficient staffing, funding, etc.

Level 4 Established districtwide materials support system.

Level 5 Integrated districtwide math/science materials and professional development center; a functioning "teacher center."

Levels of Student Assessment

Level 0 No change, no plan for change.

Level 1 Studying the issue, planning, changes driven by outside forces (new state mandates).

Level 2 Some use of alternative assessment strategies in individual schools or by teachers using inquiry-centered curriculum materials. Policy of acquiring curriculum materials that incorporate active assessment strategies.

Level 3 Systematic professional development on assessment and/or teachers developing active assessments.

Level 4 Initiating systemwide implementation of active assessment tied to grading practices and substituting for traditional, test-based grades.

Level 5 Complete implementation of districtwide active science assessment, and/or new science assessment is part of large districtwide assessment plan.

continued on next page

Five Rubrics Used to Assess the
Progress of Science Programs *continued*

Levels of Partnership Activities

Level 0 No stakeholders from the community, including scientists or engineers, are working with the district for the sole purpose of supporting its science program.

Level 1 Some stakeholders (scientists, engineers, parents, etc.) have been identified, and relationships between them and teachers or principals in some schools have been initiated. Their purposes may vary, or their involvement may be short-term or event-specific.

Level 2 Through a formal structure, district seeks to coordinate existing disparate efforts or to involve new institutions as partners to support the inquiry-centered science program.

Level 3 Partial plan for district, corporate, and/or university partnerships has been created and first steps have been initiated.

Level 4 District develops comprehensive plan with partners to secure community support and financial assistance for systemic reform.

Level 5 Plan is implemented and maintained.

Assessment Strategies
for Inquiry-Centered
Science

Key Points

▶ New assessment strategies are needed for inquiry-centered science, because traditional tests cannot assess the wide range of learning that takes place.

▶ Key strategies include pre- and post-module assessments, embedded assessments, prediction activities, and final assessments.

▶ If teachers are clear about the objective of an assessment, they will understand why a particular type of assessment is being used. For example, if a teacher wants to know whether students have learned how to design an experiment, an appropriate assessment would be to ask them to solve a problem through experimentation.

▶ Five rubrics—one for each element of the science program—can help school districts assess the progress they are making in improving their elementary science programs.

For Further Reading

Cawelti, G., ed. 1993. *Challenges and Achievements of American Education: 1993 Yearbook of the Association for Supervision and Curriculum Development.* Alexandria, Va.: Association for Supervision and Curriculum Development.

Hein, G., and S. Price. 1994. *Active Assessment for Active Science: A Guide for Elementary School Teachers.* Portsmouth, N.H.: Heinemann.

Herman, J. L., P. R. Aschbacher, and L. Winters. 1992. *A Practical Guide to Alternative Assessment.* Alexandria, Va.: Association for Supervision and Curriculum Development.

National Research Council. 1996. *National Science Education Standards.* Washington, D.C.: National Academy Press.

Raizen, S. A., J. B. Baron, A. B. Champagne, E. Haertel, I. V. Mullis, and J. Oakes. 1989. *Assessment in Elementary School Science Education.* Washington, D.C.: National Center for Improving Science Education.

Resnick, L. 1987. *Education and Learning to Think.* Washington, D.C.: National Academy Press.

Rothman, R. 1995. *Measuring Up: Standards, Assessment, and School Reform.* San Francisco: Jossey-Bass.

Shavelson, R. J., G. Baxter, and J. Pine. 1992. "Performance Assessments: Political Rhetoric and Measurement Reality." *Educational Researcher* 21 (4): 22-27.

9

Building Support for the Science Program

. . . science education partnerships are a very flexible tool for bringing rich scientific resources into the hands and minds of teachers and students.

—Art Sussman, *Science Education Partnerships*, 1993

Traditionally, public school systems have viewed themselves as insulated islands within the community. The message they have sent is, "We are the experts on education, and we know what's best for children." With the exception of parent-teacher organizations, schools usually have had little contact with the outside world.

During the 1980s and 1990s, however, some school districts have changed their views about community involvement. They now see that in times of fiscal constraints and increasing demands for scientific and technological expertise, certain sectors of the community have much to offer the schools.

For the elementary science program, community involvement is the fifth critical element in the science education reform effort. At first glance, community support may seem like an "extra," an element that, unlike curriculum and professional development, is not really crucial to the program. That perception, however, needs to be reexamined. During the early stages of program development, the more members of the community who are involved, the greater the likelihood that the program will get off to a strong start. Later on, the more stakeholders who are committed to the program, the greater the chance for its long-term survival.

This chapter will explore strategies for building support for science education reform both within the school system and in the community. The long-term goal for the science program should be to engage as many groups and organizations as possible, each of which should be seen as adding a unique value to the program.

We will begin by focusing on the school system. What can be done to gain the support of teachers, principals, and school board members? Are certain strategies particularly effective with these groups?

Then we will discuss how to build support in the community. How can parents' interest be sparked so that they become advocates for the program, both within the school and the community? How can school districts reach out to business, industry, academic institutions, museums, and other community groups that have a natural interest in improving science education in the schools?

Building Support within the School System

School districts are in a period of organizational flux. While many still depend on a central office to make key decisions about curriculum, philosophy, and pedagogy, more and more districts are decentralizing and placing more control in the hands of individual schools. For the science program, this means that teachers and principals within individual schools will be conducting their own dialogues about the direction of the science program, the role of lead teachers, and ways to integrate science with other areas of the curriculum. But even as schools strive to become more autonomous, they will continue to need the school system's support, especially if the district has established a science materials support center.

To ensure the institutionalization of the science program over the long term, all levels in the school hierarchy—teachers, principals, school system administrators, and school board officials—must be convinced of the science program's importance. Moreover, bringing disengaged teachers and administrators into the fold must be the ongoing responsibility of the program's leadership team.

Below are some strategies that have been used in school districts throughout the country. Each strategy emphasizes effective communication as the key to reaching people and building positive attitudes toward the science program.

Reaching Teachers

All effective science programs need a strong professional development component. Most school districts offer workshops to provide elementary school teachers with an opportunity to explore the concepts and skills stressed in the science modules before they introduce the modules in the classroom. Although an excellent beginning, this experience may not be enough to provide all the assistance and encouragement teachers need.

Accordingly, many school districts set aside faculty meeting time for discussion of inquiry-centered science. They have found this to be an effective way to encourage teachers to share experiences and assist one another. In their own schools, among colleagues, teachers often find it easier to express their concerns, ask questions, and "settle in" to the science program. Finally, in their own classrooms, teachers can experience the children's enthusiasm for inquiry-centered science, which is also a strong motivational force.

Teachers will become more committed to the science program when they discover that the district is committed to ensuring that the science materials will arrive in their classrooms on time. When teachers are provided with the necessary materials, have a chance to study the concepts and skills included in the science modules, and have seen how excited their students are about the program, the probability that they will engage themselves enthusiastically in the new science program rises dramatically.

Reaching Administrators and School Board Officials

In many school districts, a leadership team is the prime mover behind the science program. It often consists of school district ad-

*Many districts send staff to national conferences, such as NSRC's
Elementary Science Education Leadership Institute. These conferences
provide opportunities for information sharing and networking.*

ministrators (the science coordinator or assistant superintendent
for instruction, for example), principals, teachers, scientists, and
parents. The leadership team develops a strategic plan and works
to ensure that it is implemented.

Sometimes, however, the superintendent and his or her staff
or some school board members may be uncertain about the value
of the program. In such cases, a plan to persuade this group of
stakeholders is needed. An important first step is to provide a common and shared experience for those stakeholders who have been
identified as important to the reform effort. Such an experience
could be a visit to districts with inquiry-centered science programs
or observations of inquiry-centered classrooms on videotape.
Through such shared experiences, school district leaders will develop a new vision for science learning and a new context in which
to develop the district's strategic plan.

Another proven strategy is to give school board members and
the superintendent's staff an opportunity to experience inquiry-
centered science for themselves. Bringing materials from an inquiry-centered science module to a school board meeting, divid-
ing the members into groups, and engaging them in some of the

activities in the science module has proved to be an effective way to convince people of the importance of an inquiry-centered science program.

If time is limited, one approach to engaging this group in inquiry-centered science is to divide the science module into a series of independent investigations and to assign each investigation to a different group. After all the groups have completed their investigations, they share their findings. They discover that collectively they have explored the entire module and have been able to observe the story line unfold and the concepts build. This experience, called a *jigsaw workshop,* can be an effective way of introducing adults to inquiry-centered science education.

Building Support Within the Wider Community

Generating parent support is a first step in building support within the wider community. Many parents are influential members of the community and can be prime movers in generating enthusiasm for the program. In addition, parents are a powerful voice within schools and can exert influence over their programs through parent-teacher organizations.

Parents may also be members of the two main groups of stakeholders that can provide special assistance to the science program—university scientists and corporate leaders. As illustrated in the profiles in **Part 3: Inquiry-Centered Science in Practice,** partnerships between school districts and local universities and corporations can lead to greater political support as well as increased funding for the science program. Such relationships are crucial to the program's long-term success. At first, districts may begin with one partner, but over time, they should continue to expand the number of partners because of the unique contribution each one can make to the reform effort.

Reaching Parents

As mentioned earlier in this chapter, the local parent-teacher organization is the major vehicle through which parents participate in school activities. Because these organizations play such an active role in the schools, it is important that they be informed about the science program and encouraged to serve as advocates for it.

One way to reach parents is to make a presentation at a parent-teacher meeting. Jigsaw workshops work well with parents, too, because they allow them to experience inquiry-centered science firsthand. Once the parent organization is informed of the program, it may decide to sponsor other events, such as a family science night or a science fair. At a Family Science Night, parents work with their children on activities they have performed in science class. At science nights and science fairs, parents can see the projects their children have completed.

Creating an alliance of interested and committed parents can strengthen the science program in many ways. Some parents may be scientists, and they may offer to visit the classroom. Other parents may have access to laboratories, nature centers, or museum exhibits and could help arrange field trips to enhance the science program. Finally, parents may know community members who don't have children in the schools but who have something to offer the science program, thereby widening the scope of the program and those working on it.

Partnerships with Colleges and Universities

One goal of a school district–university partnership is to establish a means through which the scientific community can contribute to the elementary science program. Two models in California—the Pasadena Unified School District Science Program (formerly Project SEED), and San Francisco's City Science—are highlighted in Part 3 of this book. Such partnerships can be beneficial to the school district, because the university can encourage its science faculty to become involved in the program. The university may also be able to attract additional funding.

Often the best way for scientists to become involved in science education reform is by participating in professional development programs. In these settings, scientists can help broaden teachers' content knowledge of a science topic and help them better understand the rationale behind the investigations in the science modules. To do this well, scientists need to understand the challenges elementary school teachers face and the most effective ways to engage children in learning through inquiry. Once scientists view teachers as professionals, there can be a mutual exchange of ideas, leading to meaningful partnerships.

The involvement of university scientists has another benefit—the enlistment of the academic community as an advocate for science education reform within the school district and community. Many school districts have well-organized parent groups that can be very effective in maintaining district support for athletics and the arts. With appropriate support, scientists can serve the same function for the science program.

An engineer works with a student in the classroom as part of a community outreach effort.

Partnerships with Corporations

Like university partnerships, school district–corporate partnerships can bring both expertise and financial resources to the school district. Corporate sponsors may offer to help establish a materials support center, lend computer expertise, offer human resources and technical assistance, or organize professional development events such as summer institutes.

Corporate partnerships are sometimes initiated by corporations that are concerned about raising the level of scientific literacy in the nation as well as improving the quality of education in the school districts that are located in communities in which they have corporate sites. In other cases, school districts take the initiative to seek out local corporations that may have a particular interest in science education.

School district–corporate relationships usually begin in the communities where the corporation has its major plants or offices.

After deciding on where they will focus their efforts, corporations develop goals and a strategic plan for implementing their goals. For example, Hewlett-Packard has stated that one of its goals is to "improve science and mathematics proficiency significantly."[1] To realize this goal, Hewlett-Packard is collaborating with 27 school districts, mostly in the western United States, to help them improve their elementary science programs. In support of these efforts, the corporation has given grants of $30,000 per year over a three-year period to each of these school districts. However, Hewlett-Packard believes that the involvement of its employees with the school districts is more important than its financial contributions.

The Dow Chemical Company has made a commitment to work with 41 school districts near its corporate locations nationwide. In each of these locations, many Dow scientists, engineers, and other employees are working with school district personnel to introduce inquiry-centered science teaching into elementary schools.

Merck & Co., Inc., has realized its commitment to science education reform by establishing the Merck Institute for Science Education. The institute is collaborating with five school districts on the East Coast and in Kansas to establish and sustain effective inquiry-centered science programs by developing partnerships with teachers, school districts, parents, and institutions of higher education. The institute has established a resource center that is open to interested school districts. The center houses inquiry-centered curriculum modules that districts can borrow. District staff can also call the center for advice and informal technical assistance.

Bristol-Myers Squibb and DuPont, while relative newcomers to the reform effort, have already made significant contributions. Bristol-Myers Squibb is working with seven school districts. In Buffalo, New York, Bristol-Myers Squibb is contributing to the development of an effective materials support system to equip Buffalo school teachers with the supplies needed to teach inquiry-centered science. DuPont has developed a comprehensive plan and has completed the first year of implementation for the entire state of Delaware.

The Bayer Foundation has made a commitment to raising public awareness of the need for improving science literacy. In addition to working with consortia of school districts in several communities—in and around Pittsburgh, Pennsylvania; Elkhart, Indiana; and Charleston, South Carolina—Bayer has launched an extensive public relations campaign in support of science education. The campaign includes print ads, articles in local and regional newspapers and magazines, and displays in airport terminals.

School districts that are interested in initiating a corporate relationship need to prepare well before approaching the corporation. They should analyze the corporation's special concerns as well as the focus of its current philanthropic activities to determine its commitment to supporting K–12 education. As part of the research process, a spokesperson for the school district should develop a contact and begin cultivating a relationship with that person. These initial informal discussions may lead to the development of a partnership between the school district and the corporation. As the partnership evolves, it is important that both groups (the school district and the corporation) work together to develop goals and a strategic plan.

The efforts described here are only a few examples of the ways corporations are becoming involved in elementary science education reform. Numerous other partnership initiatives are under way through such groups as the Business Roundtable, local chambers of commerce, and professional societies such as the American Chemical Society, Sigma Xi, and the American Physical Society. More corporations are becoming involved, and the number of school district partnerships is increasing each year.

Partnerships with Museums

Science museums are another resource school districts can draw on as they continue to develop their science programs. In addition to providing schools with opportunities for field trips, science museums offer a broad range of resources, from space for a science materials support center to facilities for professional development. Many science museums throughout the country have outreach programs that offer teachers professional development opportunities, as well as science kits and other teaching resources that teachers can borrow.

For example, San Francisco's Exploratorium, a world-famous science museum, has provided professional development opportunities for teachers since 1972. Its programs include summer institutes for new and experienced teachers, workshops for teachers during the school year, and a lending library of science kits that can be used in conjunction with Exploratorium exhibitions.

The Buffalo Museum of Science and the Buffalo Public Schools in New York have established a partnership called TEAM 2000. The goal of the partnership is to implement an inquiry-centered science curriculum using museum-based experiences, hands-on materials, and alternative forms of assessment. Building on an earlier program funded by the National Science Foundation designed to reach 500 teachers by the fall of 1996, TEAM 2000 proposes to reach all 1,500 teachers in pre-kindergarten through grade 8 by the year 2000. The program has also made a commitment to purchase inquiry-centered science materials, which will be housed in the museum's science materials support center.

Informal Community Relationships

In addition to the formal relationships described here, there are ways for the science program to make informal connections in the community. For example, the coordinators of the science program can make presentations to civic groups, such as the Lions Club or the Junior League. If these groups are interested in learning more, they can participate in a jigsaw workshop. Another way to enlist public support is to bring some classroom science equipment and children to a local mall and present inquiry-centered science to shoppers. All of these activities can heighten awareness of the science program.

As more and more people become excited about the science program, they can be enlisted to spread the word to other members of the community. When a broad base of support has been achieved, it is a sure sign that the program has taken hold.

Key Points

▶ Building support within the school district and the wider community is essential to the success of the science program.

▶ One effective way to introduce school administrators, parents, and others to inquiry-centered science is by conducting a jigsaw workshop.

▶ Through partnerships between school districts and universities, scientists can participate in professional development programs and become advocates for science education reform in the community.

▶ Corporations can help school districts improve their science programs by forging partnerships that assist with professional development and by helping to establish science materials support centers.

▶ Science museums, too, can be effective partners in science education reform.

▶ Building multiple partnerships should be viewed as a long-term goal of the science program.

For Further Reading

Csikszentmihalyi, M. 1995. "Education for the Twenty-First Century." *Daedalus, Journal of the American Academy of Arts and Sciences* 124 (4): 107-14.

Decker, L. E., and V. A. Decker. 1988. *Home/School/Community Involvement*. Arlington, Va.: American Association of School Administrators.

Dow, P. B. 1991. *Schoolhouse Politics*. Cambridge, Mass.: Harvard University Press.

Rigden, D. W. 1992. *Business and the Schools: A Guide to Effective Programs*. New York: Council for Aid to Education.

Rigden, D. W. 1994. "Improving Science, Mathematics, and Technology Education: Opportunities for Business Support." New York: Council for Aid to Education.

Sigma Xi. 1994. *Scientists, Educators, and National Standards: Action at the Local Level.* Research Triangle Park, N.C.: Sigma Xi, The Scientific Research Society.

Sussman, A., ed. 1993. *Science Education Partnerships: Manual for Scientists and K-12 Teachers*. San Francisco: University of California, San Francisco.

Part

3

Inquiry-Centered Science in Practice

Introduction

In Parts 1 and 2, we described the rationale behind inquiry-centered science and the five elements that make up the National Science Resources Center's (NSRC) model for elementary science education reform at the district level. One question remains: Does this model work?

The answer to this question lies in **Part 3: Inquiry-Centered Science in Practice,** which explores how the model for science education reform is being implemented in communities throughout the country. We have selected eight programs that reflect the diversity of science education reform efforts nationwide. These programs are grouped under four categories.

Programs Initiated by School Districts

▶ Montgomery County Public Schools, Rockville, Maryland

▶ Spokane School District 81, Spokane, Washington

Programs Involving Corporate Partnerships

▶ East Baton Rouge Parish Public School System in partnership with the Dow Chemical Company, Midland, Michigan

▶ Cupertino Union School District in partnership with Hewlett-Packard Company, Palo Alto, California

Programs Initiated Through Partnerships with University Scientists

▶ Hands-on Science Program, Huntsville, Alabama, a consortium of school districts in partnership with the University of Alabama at Huntsville

▶ Pasadena Unified School District Science Program, formerly Project SEED (Science for Early Educational Development), in partnership with the California Institute of Technology, Pasadena, California

▶ City Science, a partnership between the University of California, San Francisco, and the San Francisco Unified School District, San Francisco, California

Programs Initiated by Consortia Serving Several School Districts

▶ Einstein Project, Green Bay, Wisconsin

These case studies illustrate several of the possible approaches for communities interested in implementing inquiry-centered science programs. Representatives of most of these programs were participants in the NSRC's Elementary Science Leadership Institute program, where they were introduced to resources, such as exemplary curriculum materials and professional development models. In addition, participants were able to benefit from the expertise of experienced science educators who had successfully introduced inquiry-centered elementary science into their school districts. These leadership experiences often proved to be turning points in the development of these programs.

The case studies demonstrate some similarities among the programs. All share a commitment to the five critical elements of an effective elementary science program. Other themes, such as the importance of leadership, the role of scientists in reform, and the contributions corporations can make, are also common threads from story to story. What varies are the pace of implementation and the relative emphasis given to particular elements.

Each story ends with a section called "Lessons Learned." These points distill what the program staff have learned from their work thus far. Our hope is that communities just starting out will benefit from the experience of others and be encouraged to move forward with their own reform efforts.

Montgomery County, Maryland

A Large Suburban School District Works to Build a Cadre of Effective Elementary Science Teachers

Culturally and economically diverse, Montgomery County Public Schools is the nation's 11th largest school district. Extending from the borders of Washington, D.C., to farmlands near Frederick, Maryland, the school district serves 63,000 elementary students in 127 schools and has about 2,600 elementary teachers responsible for teaching science. The children come from upper-middle-class neighborhoods as well as middle- and lower-income areas. The overall minority enrollment is approximately 43 percent, and students from more than 60 foreign countries are learning English as a second language.

The push for science education reform in Montgomery County began in the 1980s, when a group of community leaders expressed concern about the elementary science program. Since that time, the county has made great strides in its reform effort. The district has addressed curriculum selection, professional development, materials support, and assessment. An inquiry-centered science curriculum is in place, and the county has developed a cadre of 68 lead teachers. In addition, teachers from 90 schools have been involved in professional development activities. The program has a permanent materials support center. Finally, performance-based assessments and scoring rubrics have been created for each learning module in the science curriculum.

What happens when school administrators offer teachers state-of-the-art science materials and intensive training, as well as the guarantee that they will never have to go to the store again to buy cups, paper towels, or any other supplies for their science lessons?

In Montgomery County Public Schools, the result has been a powerful partnership between teachers and administrators that has created an exemplary inquiry-centered science program.

"We made teachers an offer they couldn't refuse," explains William McDonald, coordinator of elementary science. "We told them that not only would we give them the best curriculum materials available nationwide, but we also would make a commitment to provide intensive training in each module. As a result, they have been receptive and enthusiastic."

Indeed, professional development lies at the core of Montgomery County's science program. Everyone involved believes that the program must be driven by teachers and that only through ongoing support will teachers become expert and able to assume leadership roles among their peers. This conviction has underscored the program since its inception.

The Foundation for Reform

Montgomery County began its reform effort in 1988, when the superintendent of schools convened a task force to assess the county's K–12 science program. Under the guidance of Gerard Consuegra, then coordinator of elementary science, staff began reviewing and field-testing new curriculum materials. By 1990, staff had selected one module per grade level to place in every elementary classroom.

In 1991, the program received a boost in the form of a Teacher Enhancement Grant from the National Science Foundation (NSF). The grant enabled the county to set up an intensive professional development program while the school system made the commitment to purchase the kits needed to implement the new program. Also in 1991, Montgomery County sent a team to the National Science Resources Center Elementary Science Leadership Institute, where team members had time to plan and learn about the new curriculum modules that were available.

Team members put the information they had gained at the Leadership Institute to use almost immediately. They returned home and held their own two-week summer institute in inquiry-centered pedagogy for a cadre of 40 lead teachers as the first phase of their professional development program. This initial training was bolstered by monthly meetings held throughout the school year.

Working with science educators and scientists from the community, the lead teachers attended sessions on recent research in science education and learned about examples of science curricula in the well-established school districts of Mesa, Arizona; Anchorage, Alaska; and Schaumburg, Illinois. Lead teachers also explored such topics as the nature of science, learning theory, the constructivist approach to learning, cognitive development, integrating math and language arts into science, and cooperative learning. Training emphasized acceptance of a wide variety of learning styles and the importance of solving problems within the rigor of scientific methodology. The institute also focused on the necessity of bringing science to everyone, including children from groups typically underrepresented in the science professions—females and minorities.

Then teachers were acquainted with curriculum modules from several national curriculum projects, as well as trade books to be used in conjunction with the kits. The goal was for the lead teachers to field-test these modules in their classrooms during the 1991-92 school year.

The following school year, an additional 28 lead teachers were added to the project. All 68 lead teachers spent hours poring over curriculum materials, field-testing modules, and considering whether the materials reflected the new pedagogy and included examples of authentic assessments. Each month during the school year, they met to discuss what was happening in their classrooms. From this process, the lead teachers selected curriculum modules from a range of national curriculum programs, including Science and Technology for Children (STC), Insights, Creative Publications, and the Full Option Science System. Choosing teaching materials from an eclectic assortment of curricula has worked well in Montgomery County.

Assessment is also a key ingredient of the county's program. Teachers are working to develop assessment strategies to measure not just what students know, but also what they can do in science. Teachers are learning how to assess student attainment of science process skills through performance-based assessments, many of which are embedded in the modules themselves. In addition, final performance-based assessments and scoring rubrics have been created for each module. These assessment strategies help prepare teachers and students for the Maryland State Performance Program assessments, which are given at the end of grades 3 and 5.

Implementing an Ambitious Professional Development Plan

By 1993, the lead teachers and NSF project staff were prepared to begin their ambitious training effort. Their goal was for the lead teachers to train 280 teachers from 18 schools in 1993 and 560 teachers from 31 schools in 1994. The plan is to train all Montgomery County elementary science teachers by the 1997-98 school year.

Working in conjunction with Thomas DuMars, NSF project specialist for the county, the lead teachers conduct a week-long summer institute similar to the one they attended. During the institute, teachers receive an initial overview of the new modules; then they break into small groups by grade level, where they have an opportunity to work closely with their peers and with the experienced lead teachers.

"The teachers benefit from the camaraderie of the other teachers," says Wanda Coates, a third-grade lead teacher. "When they go back to the classroom, they experience a high level of success."

But the training doesn't stop after the summer institute. Teachers receive three units throughout the year in 12-week cycles. Before receiving any materials to support the module, all participating teachers are released from class for a half day of training in the new module. Halfway through the teaching cycle, teachers also attend an after-school support meeting. The purpose of these meetings, Coates explains, is for teachers to go beyond the initial training and discuss ways to extend the experiences, as well as to discuss any problems teachers may be experiencing.

"Even teachers who are reluctant to teach science are able to follow the directions and complete the lessons," says Celeste King, a fifth-grade lead teacher. "As a result, teachers who never taught science are now doing it."

The literature on professional development makes a strong case for ongoing discussions among peers. What makes this possible in Montgomery County is the high degree of administrative support for the efforts. Participating schools release teachers so that they can attend these meetings. In addition, teachers can now receive science content credit for attending the summer institutes. These benefits provide added incentives for teachers new to inquiry-centered science to attend the meetings and institutes.

Teachers aren't the only group that needs administrative support to make a contribution to inquiry-centered science. Principals also need to be informed about the new teaching strategies. "Principals were telling me that they also needed opportunities to get together and talk," says McDonald. "We decided to include them more."

So, starting with the summer institute held in 1995, the county offered its first science training for principals. During the institute and four follow-up meetings held during the 1995-96 school year, principals were given much-needed information about the new pedagogy and the science modules. The result has been more knowledgeable principals who are better equipped to observe teachers engaged in inquiry-centered science and to offer constructive advice and criticism.

Bringing Scientists on Board

Recently, the project has added a new dimension to training—scientists. Through a partnership with the American Physical Society, Montgomery County is working with 45 scientists who have been trained to work with elementary school teachers. After attending a day-long workshop where scientists are alerted to the issues facing elementary school teachers, the kinds of curriculum materials they are using, and the role they can play in training, scientists volunteer their time by participating in workshops designed to introduce teachers to inquiry-centered modules. In that setting, scientists join teachers as learners, model inquiry, and validate science as an interesting way to explore the world.

"Science is inquiry," says Ramon Lopez, the director of education and outreach programs for the American Physical Society and the creator of the program. "Give scientists materials and they are off asking questions and experimenting. We try to instill the same spirit into the teachers."

In addition to serving as a model for the pedagogy behind inquiry-centered science, scientists can answer teachers' questions about content. Lopez recalls a moment during the meeting on the STC module *Electric Circuits* when several of the teachers were puzzled by a phenomenon they had noticed while making a model of a light bulb using nichrome wire. The teachers had observed that if the nichrome wire was too long, the bulb did not glow. They wondered why.

"That's a great question for physicists," says Lopez, "and they provided a good, simple explanation. The teachers then responded by discussing how they could use the information to extend the activity. It was a perfect example of professionals interacting and providing expertise from their respective areas."

Establishing a Science Materials Support Center

As part of Montgomery County's commitment to teachers, program leaders established a science materials support center within the first two years of the program. As in many school districts around the country, it was a challenge to find a space large enough for such a facility. The materials center has already been housed in three different spots. Now, however, it has found a permanent home in an unused elementary school building in the western part of the county. DuMars runs the materials center.

"There's a lot to do," DuMars says. "The logistics of picking up kits and delivering them requires planning, not to mention constructing kits and replenishing those that come back from the teachers."

One of DuMars's biggest discoveries is the importance of bidding to get the best deals. "The big wholesale suppliers will help you keep your prices down," he says. "And it is far cheaper to construct your own kits than to buy the materials from the publishers." By cheap, DuMars means about $3 per child for refurbishing for a whole year. And buying consumables, such as different kinds of liquids, in bulk is another way to save money on some of the more expensive items.

To help pack, ship, and refurbish approximately 3,100 kits three times a year, DuMars depends on four full-time employees for assistance. Currently, there are enough kits available for 150 teachers to teach a module simultaneously.

Does the system work perfectly? No. Are there problems? Of

course. But on the whole, teachers get the supplies when they need them so that they can teach science on time.

"Teachers need to be educated, too," says DuMars. "Our teachers have a tendency to hold on to the kits, which jams up the system. When the 12 weeks are up, we need to have the kits back."

The project also realized that the support of secretaries and building service workers is critical in getting the kits in and out of schools on time. To help enlist this support, DuMars implemented training for these individuals during the summer institute and maintains direct contact with them throughout the year.

Plans for the Future

In less than a decade, Montgomery County has evolved from a district depending largely on textbooks to one using materials as a springboard for inquiry-centered learning. Although the district has come a long way, much work remains to be done. Even with an intensive professional development program in place, many teachers have yet to be introduced to the science modules. And those using the modules would like to reach the point where they can tailor the science module to the interests of their class.

Montgomery County is also working to take greater advantage of computer technology to enhance student learning in science. For example, the county is working toward creating a districtwide telecommunications network, which will enable students to transmit collected data and conclusions to their peers at other schools. Some schools in the county already have this capacity. Students are also using graphing software in their investigations and experimenting with specially designed cameras, which offer innovative ways for students to communicate what they have learned and to create student portfolios.

To continue to grow professionally so that they can use innovative curricula and technology effectively, many teachers would like additional training. "The training I have received is sufficient, but it is not enough," says King. "I would like to have a stronger science background so I can answer my students' questions more completely."

"We would all welcome additional training," says McDonald. "Our goal is to raise all our teachers to the next level."

Lessons Learned

▶ Teachers need support and extensive professional development to be prepared to teach inquiry-centered science effectively.

▶ Operating an efficient science materials support center is difficult. Teachers must assist materials support center staff by returning their kits on time.

▶ Involvement of principals and building staff is critical to the success of the program.

Spokane, Washington

A City School District Struggles to Put the Pieces Together

Spokane is a socioeconomically diverse community located in the eastern part of Washington State, close to the Idaho border. The school district has 35 elementary schools (K–6) and 800 elementary school teachers, and it serves 17,850 elementary school students. The population of the district is largely Caucasian, with some Native Americans, Asians, and African Americans.

The impetus for reform in Spokane District 81 came from school administrators within the district. The district's major focus to date has been on curriculum selection, professional development, and science materials support. The district has a module-based, inquiry-centered science curriculum, and the majority of the district's teachers have been involved in professional development activities. The district has established a science materials support center, but it has been difficult to organize and maintain the center.

"**D**o the same creatures live in the little Spokane River as in the pond near my house?" asked a fifth-grader in Lorna Spear's class in Spokane's School District 81. "How can we find out?"

This question emerged from work on the module *Microworlds,* a Science and Technology for Children life science unit in the district's new inquiry-centered science program. The philosophy behind the inquiry-centered approach is that as much as possible, children's interests and questions drive classroom discussions.

In response to that question, Spear organized a series of field trips to try to find out what kinds of organisms live in rivers and ponds. The class collected specimens at both sites and took them back to the classroom, where they examined them under a microscope. They discovered that different organisms live in different bodies of water, and they concluded that this was largely due to the unique characteristics of each river and pond.

Spear, a lead teacher in Spokane's science program, believes that children need freedom to learn, so throughout the day, she gives them many choices. As a result, children spend time working in groups and alone, reading, and conducting scientific investigations. Spear has found that "children are more self-initiated and creative without my intervention."

"All types of learning are welcome in my classroom," explains Spear. "Another little boy was interested in exploring how the earth started spinning. We brainstormed about the problem in class. Then I encouraged him to go home and read about it. He came back to class with the same explanation that astronomers have come up with—that the big bang set everything in motion and gravity creates the pull among planets."

Planning the Science Program

Learning experiences like these become possible when a school district makes the commitment to implement an inquiry-centered program. Under the direction of Science Coordinator Scott Stowell, Spokane's science program is now entering its seventh year. Stowell and his colleagues used much of the information gathered at the 1989 National Science Resources Center Elementary Science Leadership Institute to develop a comprehensive K–6 science action plan.

The first phase of the plan called for an in-depth curriculum review and development process. According to teacher Jane Gorder-Harrison, the Leadership Institute made it "crystal clear" that a kit-based program was the best approach. The science committee spent long hours wrestling with the topics to be covered in the curriculum, getting input from teachers, and developing a comprehensive curriculum matrix made up of life science, physical science, and earth science strands, with special emphasis on environmental issues and technology. Once the strands were established, the district invited representatives from many companies to visit and present their products. The district piloted many modules, rejected some, accepted others, and ultimately filled in the curriculum matrix with modules from several national companies as well as some developed at the district level.

Professional Development Activities

As the modules were being selected, Spokane's professional development program also began to take shape. In June 1992, the district and its partners, Eastern Washington University and Partners-at-Large, a coalition of business, industry, and government agencies, received a five-year National Science Foundation Teacher Enhancement Grant. Stowell and Robert Gibbs, a physicist from Eastern Washington University, were named co-directors of the grant.

The following month, Stowell and Gibbs held the district's first summer institute for lead teachers. The institute lasted four weeks and provided professional development activities for 75 district teachers and 20 teachers from private schools. The institute's sessions were conducted jointly by classroom teachers and university scientists. The participating teachers now make up the cadre of lead teachers, who, along with school principals, work with teachers new to inquiry-centered science.

For the first three years of the project, typical staff development consisted of either two 10-hour sessions of intensive study of two modules or attendance at the 30-hour summer institute. The fact that teachers were given a choice proved to be popular with teachers and a real strength of the program. In both settings, teachers worked in groups and progressed through the lessons in a module, just as their students would do. Instructors modeled appropriate instructional strategies, such as implementing the learning cycle and asking different kinds of questions. The summer institute also explored other issues related to science education reform, including learning theory and assessment. Teachers appreciated the presence of knowledgeable university scientists and the opportunity to ask questions and learn more about the subject matter.

During the summer of 1993, 15 elementary schools sent 93 teachers to the second summer institute, where lead teachers conducted many of the grade-level workshops. Gorder-Harrison, one of the summer institute instructors, recalls that "teachers start to act like kids; they can't keep their hands off the materials." The teachers' interest and enthusiasm soon spread to educators in schools not yet involved in the program.

In fact, interest in the school district was so high that the remaining 20 schools in the district requested that they be brought into the program the following year instead of being phased in over a two-year period as originally planned. The administrators agreed.

Science Materials Support—The Critical Element

The decision to grant the schools' request was to create unforeseen problems in another area of the program—the science materials support center. Indeed, creating a workable materials support center is one of the real challenges facing school districts engaged in reform. A district such as Spokane, which serves 800 elementary school teachers, must supply kits to the schools, refurbish them, keep track of inventory, and pick the kits up on time. Although district leaders made every effort to plan up front and to consider every detail in the structuring of the program, sometimes circumstances make implementation difficult.

"Bringing in 20 schools in one year was too much," says Stowell. "We didn't have the space we needed or the personnel to serve that many schools. All the details need to be thought out carefully in advance."

The problems fell into several categories. One was space. A warehouse formerly used to store textbooks had been designated to house the kits. But the textbooks had not been removed in a timely fashion, so there wasn't enough room for the kits. The reason this situation arose can be traced to some of the challenges inherent in the process of planning and implementing a massive reform effort.

"We had some changes in personnel," Stowell says. "I had been working closely with the assistant superintendent on this project, but he retired. New individuals came on board who were not familiar with the logistical support that was needed. They were very supportive, but I guess I didn't articulate all the details clearly enough for them during the transition. As a result, the pace of moving the old textbooks out was not quick enough."

The jurisdiction for the science materials support center did not fall solely under Stowell's supervision, which compounded the problem. While Stowell coordinated the scheduling of the science kits, another department was responsible for operations at the science materials support center. So the issue became one of communicating the need to that office and solving the problem in collaboration with key individuals from other departments within the school district.

Problem Solving Is the Key

At this point, the district moved into a problem-solving mode. It had commissioned a study of the materials support center in the summer of 1994 to obtain all the information needed to get it up and running. Using the study's report as a guide, the district brought in Robyn Norwood, an experienced manager, to supervise the center.

"We completely reorganized the space," she says. "We took the books off the shelves and made room for the kits. Once we had room to see what supplies we had, we could see what supplies we needed to order."

To keep track of the vast number of supplies, from beakers to bottles, wires to bells, tuning forks to radios, the staff at the materials center developed an inventory sheet. The inventory sheet ensured that the kits would be ready when the teachers needed them.

Along with keeping track of the inventory, Norwood and Stowell developed a workable pickup and delivery schedule. Instead of having all the kits delivered on an eight-week cycle, Stowell put them on six-, seven-, and eight-week cycles. That way, the staff at the center could refurbish one group of kits while another group was out with the teachers. The schedule also carefully delineated which teachers were to receive kits during specific time periods.

With the inventory and schedule in place, Norwood then tackled the issue of routing. Using the district's delivery system, she developed a routing system where geographical quadrants were served on a Monday-Thursday and Tuesday-Friday rotation system. Teachers who had requested kits knew exactly when to expect them and where to pick them up. Implementing this schedule kept the kits moving through the system smoothly.

Spokane's experience underscores how critical a science materials center is to the success of the science program. There are many details to attend to, and it is easy to overlook one or two essential ones. When that happens, it doesn't take long for problems to occur. The key to success is a well-thought-out plan and strong management at the science materials support center.

Moving Forward

With the science materials support center problems under control, science program staff are looking forward to a smooth road ahead. The teachers, too, have had additional time to fine-tune the skills they acquired during the professional development programs. The lead teachers as well as classroom teachers have been given the option of participating in advanced workshops. Also, a subcommittee consisting of the original lead teachers has begun to identify the essential learning goals for each module and to correlate them with the goals defined in state and national standards.

Many teachers, however, are still struggling to learn the basics. Co-Director Gibbs observed that much of the initial training focused on "nitty-gritty" issues of materials management, classroom management, and understanding the activities in the modules. Few teachers have reached the "expert" level, where they are able to modify the modules, integrate them with other parts of the curriculum, and bring in other materials to enhance the kits. Although lead teacher Lorna Spear agrees, she also notes that the program "has given teachers support and more time to talk to one another." Fostering collegial relationships among teachers is one of the goals of the project and provides a way for teachers to grow professionally.

At this point, however, Gibbs says that "we have been able to bring most of our teachers to the level of mechanical use. That shouldn't be perceived as negative. What it means is that we are teaching science significantly better than we were before."

Lessons Learned

▶ The implementation process needs to be planned carefully. The pace of implementation should not accelerate beyond the school district's capacity to meet the needs of the teachers who will be participating in the program.

▶ The establishment of a well-functioning science materials support center is critical. Teachers can't teach inquiry-centered science without all of the necessary materials.

▶ Science program staff must be realistic about the goals of the professional development program. Most teachers will need to pass through a period of "mechanical use" before they master all the fine points of inquiry-centered science teaching.

East Baton Rouge Parish, Louisiana

Corporate Partnership and an Emphasis on Strong Professional Development Spearhead Reform Efforts

The East Baton Rouge Parish School System includes 64 K–5 elementary schools. There are approximately 40,000 students and 1,200 teachers in those schools. East Baton Rouge's science program has focused on professional development and devising effective assessments of student learning. The program has been strengthened by a corporate partnership with the Dow Chemical Company.

Sheila Emonet, a fourth-grade teacher at Lanier Elementary School, is a 1995 Presidential Award recipient who has earned national recognition for excellence in teaching science. Around East Baton Rouge, however, she's best known as the teacher who "does those bones."

A second-grade unit on bones and skeletons may be Emonet's greatest claim to local fame, but her interest in inquiry-based science is broad and long-standing. Mignon Morgan, science specialist for the parish, cites Emonet as a pioneer in science education reform in the area. Long before science kits became available, Emonet was bringing materials into her science classroom to spark students' interest. Asked to describe the strength of hands-on learning, she says, "It's not just me giving you information. Instead, the idea is 'Let's learn together.' I make the learning mine as well."

Emonet has taught for 10 years. Across the parish at Tanglewood Elementary School, Clydette Rispone, who has taught for five years, was also a hands-on science teacher in the days when enterprising teachers made their own science kits. She found teaching materials just about everywhere; for example, she collected seashells at neighborhood garage sales. On her first day as a student teacher, she prompted a brainstorming activity for a new module on *Water, Air, and Weather* by bringing a fighting fish to class. Why take the trouble? "Hands-on activities," she states with conviction, "bring science to life."

Good Teachers: Born or Made?

The enterprising spirit of Emonet and Rispone might make it appear that good teachers are born, not made. While some traits may be innate, every teacher needs support and ongoing learning opportunities. For this reason, Morgan speaks with special pride of the parish's staff development program. All teachers must have at least three hours of experiential training with a new science module before they can check the kit out of the Science Resource Center. That training is provided by master teachers from the system's own staff.

"For the first two years that we used the kits," Morgan recalls, "we invited in company representatives or other professionals. They made wonderful presentations. The teachers were enthusiastic. But three weeks later, they'd come to me and say, 'Mignon, I'm not sure I can do it myself.'"

As a result, the training for each module in East Baton Rouge today is done by teachers who have used the kit at least once in their own classrooms. Approximately 10 teachers attend each of the day-long sessions. It's a thorough process. "We start," Morgan notes, "by opening the box." Working in pairs or groups, the teachers go through every activity in the module. They not only learn about the kits, they also have an opportunity to network with other teachers in their school system. Equally important, they meet a local resource person to whom they can turn when questions arise.

Another component of staff development is provided through a five-year Teacher Enhancement Grant from the National Science Foundation (NSF). The grant, awarded in 1993, targets teachers in kindergarten through third grade and focuses on the physical sciences. Through this program, the parish has developed a cadre of 32 mentor teachers in 16 schools. During the summer of 1993, the mentor candidates, which included Rispone, earned graduate credit in physical science. Once the school year began, a team of science specialists, including a consultant in assessment,

visited their classrooms weekly to model effective teaching and to
provide feedback to the mentors-in-training. The teachers also attended monthly seminars at the Science Resource Center. The
same basic framework, consisting of summer graduate work and
training during the school year, continued in 1993-94.

To launch the second phase of this capacity-building effort,
the system selected 34 lead teachers in 1995. After two weeks of
summer training, each lead teacher was paired with a mentor
teacher at the same grade level in another school. The two teachers then continued to work together for an entire year. The mentors model effective teaching practices; the lead teachers try out
new techniques and receive feedback.

"Our Whole Thinking Has Changed"

For Rispone, participation in the mentoring program was an irre-
placeable experience. "Our minds work differently," she says. "Our
whole thinking has changed."

Student assessment is one area where changes in thinking are
most evident. Although hard data on student achievement are still
being collected and analyzed for purposes of the NSF grant, teachers see the advantages of hands-on learning almost daily.

Emonet's experience with assessment has revealed "obvious differences" between hands-on science and traditional textbook science.
Students who have engaged in hands-on learning are more enthusiastic and have more positive attitudes toward science. Differences in
written test results are less dramatic. Nonetheless, hands-on science is
miles ahead of the game. "We're doing more writing," Emonet explains, "and the students have to record results and write in their
journals when they study electricity. In a hands-on classroom," she
quickly adds, "the students *also* have to construct an electric switch."

Cooperation with the Dow Chemical Company

The Dow Chemical Company, a major employer in East Baton
Rouge, has been instrumental in the progress achieved in the system in both science and mathematics. As Morgan puts it, "They've
been tremendous." Dow offered an initial $15,000 grant to East
Baton Rouge in 1992. The company made a commitment to provide
$40,000 annually for the next five years to purchase and refurbish

science kits and to provide other learning resources. Sue Blanchard, Dow's training coordinator for human resources, was a member of the four-person team that attended the National Science Resources Center (NSRC) Elementary Leadership Institute in 1992, and she remains actively involved in the program. Accountability is an important feature of the successful relationship that has been established between Dow and school district leaders, she notes. The school submits an activity report to the corporate offices yearly, and progress is jointly evaluated.

The groundwork for such collaboration began in the early 1990s, when Dow, Exxon Corporation, and Louisiana State University (LSU) formed a public-private alliance for the purpose of preventing overlap in corporate support for school programs. Representatives of Shell Oil Company, Ethyl Corporation, and the local chamber of commerce soon joined the alliance. Today, the alliance is working with 10 of the state's 64 parishes. Alliance members meet with science and math supervisors monthly. The result, Blanchard notes with satisfaction, is that "we're beginning to see much more cooperation among the school districts." If, for example, there are one or two unfilled spots in a training program offered by East Baton Rouge, teachers from West Baton Rouge and Iberville Parishes are invited to fill them. These "win-win" arrangements ensure that staff development is as cost-effective as possible. The alliance is also exploring the use of the Internet and America Online for staff training.

LSU's Louisiana Energy and Environmental Resources and Information Center (LEERIC) has played an active role in science education reform in the system and throughout the state. LEERIC staff member Emily Young was a member of the 1992 NSRC Leadership Institute team. LEERIC functioned as the materials center for three parishes during the first year of the program, and it continues to serve West Baton Rouge and Iberville. LEERIC staff provide supplementary teaching materials on request. They also provide a custom-made list of resource books, trade books, and videotapes in each science kit.

A Balancing Act

Maintaining a large and rapidly growing program with multiple funding sources requires the creative use of resources. For example, the NSF grant provides training for teachers in grades K–3 only, so the system must find additional support for training of a similarly high caliber for fourth- and fifth-grade teachers. Moreover, the NSF grant covers only the physical sciences, yet the science curriculum already includes earth and life sciences.

Having a major role in ensuring that resources are well allocated and gaps are overcome is Lola Soileau, science supervisor and principal investigator for the NSF grant. Soileau is an advocate for elementary school science with the board of education, which allocates funds to cover the cost of kits and supplies that exceed the resources provided by Dow. In a time of fiscal constraints, Soileau and her staff must balance science education reform goals with a dose of realism. "It may not happen in five years," she admits.

But it *will* happen. Signs of progress are everywhere. One in four elementary school teachers has been trained in at least one science module, and four different hands-on modules are being used at each grade level. The Science Resource Center is swamped with requests; each kit is used four or five times yearly. At the halfway point of its five-year plan, the East Baton Rouge system has made major strides in implementing elementary science education reform.

Lessons Learned

▶ Local teachers understand their colleagues' needs. Appropriately trained, they are often more effective in leading staff development programs than are publishers' sales representatives.

▶ Mentoring programs that match a lead teacher with a less-experienced teacher in the same school are a practical and effective means of promoting individual teacher development.

▶ Alliances between the public and private sectors, especially when they benefit from a strong corporate presence, can be instrumental in promoting science education reform.

Cupertino, California

A Small School District Builds a Strong Corporate Partnership

The Cupertino Union School District serves students residing in a 26-square-mile area of northern California that includes the City of Cupertino and parts of Los Altos, San Jose, Santa Clara, Saratoga, and Sunnyvale. The district's 19 elementary schools have an enrollment of 14,500 and a teaching staff of 523.

The major focus of the Cupertino Union School District has been on curriculum selection, professional development, and building community support. The district selected an inquiry-centered science curriculum and instituted a comprehensive professional development program. Through a strong partnership with Hewlett-Packard, both teachers and students have benefited from the expertise of scientists.

In the summer of 1992, Marybarbara Zorio and her teammates came to the National Science Resources Center's (NSRC) Elementary Science Leadership Institute prepared to meet new challenges. "We had the new *California Science Framework* under one arm and blank newsprint paper under the other," she recalls. Zorio herself had been named district science resource teacher only two days earlier.

The Cupertino team was not starting from scratch. The district had already initiated hands-on science in some of its elementary schools. It had a longstanding commitment to staff development. Equally important, the science program had strong backing from a corporate partner, the Hewlett-Packard Company. Under the Hewlett-Packard–Cupertino partnership, which began in 1987, 70 Hewlett-Packard mathematicians and scientists visited students and teachers in two different schools every week. Hewlett-Packard also offered science classes to Cupertino teachers and administrators. And in 1992, Hewlett-Packard awarded the district a three-year grant that would provide $30,000 per year for the elementary science program. The district decided to earmark these funds for staff development.

Mark Butler, a Hewlett-Packard scientist and member of the Leadership Institute team, recalls the enthusiasm shared by his teammates early on. "It was a great kickoff for the whole program," he recalls. Even though Hewlett-Packard had been involved in science education reform in Cupertino for many years, it was in the team-building environment of the Institute that the members were able to "bond" and the program gained momentum.

Taking Steps Toward Science Education Reform

At the Institute, Zorio, Butler, and their teammates drafted a three-year plan for science education reform. "It wasn't written in cement. Sometimes we had to change course," Zorio admits, "but we had a road along which we were moving." The plan had a dual function: to meet local needs as well as the criteria set forth in the newly issued *California Framework.*

A first step in the plan was to develop a system for introducing the key science content areas. Cupertino decided to focus first on the physical sciences; life science and earth science would be introduced in years 2 and 3, respectively. A second step was to select the curricula. The *California Framework* recommended five elementary science programs, including the NSRC's Science and Technology for Children (STC) program. The district invited representatives of these programs to make presentations concerning their products. Selected modules were pilot-tested in winter 1993. Working as partners, two teachers—a veteran science teacher and a less-experienced, "science-shy" teacher—taught each of the modules under consideration for adoption. The experiences of the two teachers combined, Zorio noted, gave the team the needed "rounded perspective."

Staff Development: "The Power Has to Come from Within"

Staff development might be described as the linchpin of science education reform in Cupertino. The district's staff development plan, initiated well in advance of classroom implementation of hands-on science, is centered on learning by example. Teachers have the opportunity to experience the kinds of instruction they are expected to provide to their students.

All of Cupertino's elementary school teachers had that experiential opportunity on September 26, 1994, when Cupertino held its first districtwide Science Learning Day. Teachers who had pilot-tested the kits chosen for inclusion in the curriculum conducted walk-throughs of the materials for their colleagues who would be presenting those modules in their classrooms in the fall. In all, 13 different kits in the physical sciences were presented. The event was highly successful, and a second Science Learning Day was scheduled for May 1995.

One reason for the success of this event is that the planners tapped expertise among the teachers. "The power of staff development has to come from within," Zorio comments. This approach has an added advantage: it is cost-effective. Teachers familiar with the kits can replicate the sessions for their colleagues throughout the year at convenient times, and they are close at hand for follow-up consultations.

John Erkman, director of instruction since 1993, maintains that the approach being used in training teachers in science fits well within the district's overall staff development model. "We have a commitment to make sure we give our teachers the best content knowledge balanced with the opportunities for coaching, peer support, reflection, and practice that have to be in place to make the content integral to the classroom experience," he says.

Elementary science education reform, the Cupertino planners know, is much more than using kits and getting students involved in hands-on activities. In Erkman's words, "It's bringing questioning and discovery into the classroom. Our teachers must shift from being the 'fountain of knowledge' into being people who guide the students in finding information. If our teachers are going to make that shift, we've got to do more than simply say, 'Go ahead and do this.'"

Mentor teacher Patti Holcomb, previously counted among the "science-shy," attests to the impact of Cupertino's staff development program and the paradigm shift to which Erkman refers. "The focus of our training," she recalls, "was to make us more comfortable with our general knowledge of science. Part of this is realizing that we don't need to have all the answers. What we *do* need to know is where to go to find them."

The Hewlett-Packard Partnership: "More than Money Alone"

The financial support of the Hewlett-Packard Company was instrumental in getting the Cupertino program off to a strong start, and the district recently received a second Hewlett-Packard grant. Nonetheless, in Zorio's words, it's been "more than money alone" when it comes to the importance of Hewlett-Packard in helping the district realize its science education goals.

For example, Hewlett-Packard consultants helped the district design its materials center, where the science kits are stored. They also set up classroom computers and are information resources for Holcomb and others. When a difficult question arises in a module in STC's *Magnets and Motors* unit, Holcomb's fifth-graders can communicate on-line with Hewlett-Packard staff. Because of this close collaboration with a technology-based company, says Holcomb, the students "don't feel like they're outside of science. They like the feeling of being in the middle, rather than being on the outside looking in."

When the corporate partnership began, Hewlett-Packard gave Mark Butler full-time responsibility for serving as a liaison between the school system and the company. His job is to match Hewlett-Packard resources with learning needs. One of the most productive matches has involved Chuck Morehouse, a Hewlett-Packard physical scientist. As part of Cupertino's "Afternoon with the Science Expert" program, Morehouse has met monthly with fifth-grade teachers who are teaching *Magnets and Motors*. A second physical scientist is slated to help out in a similar fashion with the STC first-grade module *Solids and Liquids*.

Morehouse is a central resource for all teachers. Under a new program, Science Partners, that began in the 1994-95 academic year, Hewlett-Packard scientists volunteer to work with individual teachers in their classrooms on a one-on-one basis. Eight Cupertino schools were involved in Science Partners during its first year. Following a successful pilot test, the project, Butler notes, will be "rolled out" so that there will be at least three or four scientists in each of the district's 19 elementary schools. Hewlett-Packard has also introduced the program in other school districts.

A Broadening Circle of Support

At the NSRC Leadership Institute, the Cupertino team gained an understanding of the importance of community involvement. Consequently, the district formed two community task forces. The groups tackled important questions such as, What does the community value in science education? and What can we do to provide that to students? Both groups have become solid advocates for science education reform—especially important resources in an era of budget cutbacks.

Community scientists have also been drawn into the action; for example, an environmental scientist from the City of Cupertino recently visited a classroom to help students with a composting activity. The partnership established with Hewlett-Packard has thus been complemented by a broadening community partnership in Cupertino. Erkman sums it up like this: "Our teachers have multiple layers of support—from mentors, lead teachers, and community scientists."

By building an effective corporate partnership and focusing on staff development, Cupertino has developed a broad base of support for its elementary science program. This has enabled the school district to create an elementary science program that meets exacting state standards, provides its students with challenging opportunities in science education, and boasts a cadre of enthusiastic, well-informed, and well-equipped teachers.

Lessons Learned

▶ Creative corporate partnerships with school districts can provide opportunities for engineers and scientists to become directly involved in school science programs.

▶ School districts can tap local expertise by giving their own experienced staff responsibility for professional development. This increases the probability that staff will be enthusiastic about the program, and it is also cost-effective.

▶ Community task forces can offer a rich source of input into planning efforts and broaden the base of support in the community.

Huntsville, Alabama

A University–School District Partnership Creates a Multidistrict Program Step by Step

The Hands-on Activity Science Program is a joint venture of the University of Alabama at Huntsville and the following seven local school districts: Athens, Decatur, Fort Payne, Huntsville, Madison County, Morgan County, and Scottsboro. A total of 89 elementary schools, 1,665 teachers, and 41,850 students participate in the science program.

Planners of the Huntsville program have emphasized curriculum selection, professional development, and materials support. A module-based inquiry-centered science curriculum is in place, and program coordinators have worked hard to cultivate a cadre of leader master teachers. A consortium-based materials support center serving the seven participating school districts has also been established.

John Wright has had an eclectic career. A scientist, university professor, and former college president, he now has a new calling. As project investigator of the Hands-on Activity Science Program (HASP), a joint venture of the University of Alabama at Huntsville and seven school districts, Wright is a crusader in the nationwide effort to bring inquiry-centered science to elementary school children.

Fortunately, the project has received lots of help. HASP began as a partnership with the local chamber of commerce, the Marshall Space Flight Center, and the University of Alabama at Huntsville. Representatives from each of these groups met with school representatives to determine how they could improve the quality of precollege science education. The project received an initial boost when it obtained an Industry/School Partnership Grant from the National Science Foundation (NSF) in 1990. The collaboration was further strengthened by the formation of the Institute for Science Education, also in 1990. The institute is housed at the university.

The institute operates under the premise that the university will share its resources as part of its commitment to improving pre-college science education. As Frank Franz, president of the University of Alabama at Huntsville, explains, "The Institute for Science Education provides a linkage between the university and K–12 education. The science program offers an important public service and engages the university with the community."

As an experienced administrator, Wright brings to the reform movement essential leadership qualities that enable him to build on a strong base of community and administrative support. "I was comfortable talking to superintendents and corporate executives," recalls Wright. "And we called the state Department of Education when we needed their support."

A Vision for Science Education Reform

The reason superintendents and state education officials found the HASP team so persuasive was that its members had articulated a vision for science education reform. Attendance at the 1991 National Science Resources Center (NSRC) Elementary Science Leadership Institute was of key importance in the development of this vision. Knowledge acquired at the Institute irrevocably changed the course of Huntsville's program.

The Institute, Wright recalls, helped the team "reformulate and crystallize" its thinking. As a result, the team reevaluated some key parts of its action plan. "We originally saw hands-on science instruction as a way to supplement our science curriculum," Wright recalls. But the experience convinced Wright and his colleagues that effective science reform would require replacing the existing curriculum with an inquiry-centered science program.

The decision to change to an inquiry-centered program also meant another important step: developing a module-based curriculum program. Before they attended the NSRC's Leadership Institute, Wright and his colleagues from Huntsville were not aware that modules were available in the marketplace. In fact, they had assumed that they would have to create the modules themselves.

"We had already arranged for teams of scientists and teachers to begin working," recalls Arlene Childers, HASP associate director. But after reviewing materials at the Institute, the team went home and spent the year assisting school districts as they piloted modules in local classrooms. The program is now built around a combination of modules from the Science and Technology for Children (STC) program, Insights, and the Full Option Science System (FOSS) program.

Establishing the Materials Center

While teachers were developing the program's curriculum matrix, HASP team members were working on another key component of an effective elementary science program: a central materials center. To determine the most effective way to begin, the HASP team involved both teachers and engineers in the planning process. Teachers visited a materials center in Mesa, Arizona, and a team of engineers and teachers conducted a study on the best way to distribute and refurbish the materials. The consensus from both groups was that a central system was the most efficient way to deal with the materials component of HASP's elementary science program.

To implement this recommendation, HASP started a materials center in the Huntsville Chamber of Commerce building; later, the center moved to the university. While the university provided the space, Huntsville and Madison County agreed to use their districts' transportation systems to deliver modules to the schools. With that partnership in place, HASP adopted a consortium model. The program charges participating school districts approximately $6 per student per year to refurbish the kits. In addition, each participating school district pays a flat fee of $300 per teacher per year; this money is used to build the inventory of modules.

This system has been highly successful. The consortium has worked so well that five additional school districts—Decatur, Athens, Fort Payne, Scottsboro, and Morgan Counties—have joined since the materials center opened in 1991. "Establishing a materials center is a critical element that people may wish to ignore," says Wright. " But it is crucial to the success of the program."

Creating a Cadre of Leader Master Teachers

As in many school districts engaged in reform throughout the country, professional development is a key element in HASP's elementary science program. HASP has enjoyed continuous support from NSF for its professional development programs. Between 1993 and 1995, HASP had a Teacher Enhancement Grant. The goal of this project was to train 126 Leader Master Teachers (LMTs) who would assume leadership roles in their schools. The teachers' training took place at a three-week summer institute and at sessions conducted midway through the teaching of a module. Topics covered at the training sessions included classroom management, science content related to the selected modules, constructivist learning theory and the learning cycle, and the use of questioning strategies designed to develop higher-order thinking skills.

"We had our first training in *The Life Cycle of Butterflies,* which created excitement for both teachers and kids," says Joy Drummond, a second-grade LMT in the Huntsville City Schools. "The kids were beside themselves, they loved it so much. Their enthusiasm captured the teachers' imaginations and made them excited as well."

In the early days of the program, familiarizing the teachers with the modules and generating excitement were the chief priorities. Tereasa Rollings, science coordinator from Madison County Schools and one of the original teacher trainers, recalls, "When the first group of teachers came to the initial training session, many lacked science content knowledge. They were particularly anxious about the physical science modules."

Time and experience with the modules have helped ease their concerns. After receiving intensive training, teachers have become much more comfortable teaching inquiry-centered science. Rollings notes that "teachers are using the new questioning strategies and the four-stage learning cycle in other areas of the curriculum. They have become used to children moving around the classroom and working together in cooperative groups. And teachers are discovering that integrating science with language arts and other curriculum areas gives them enough time to teach all the subjects."

Pam Patrick, an LMT at the kindergarten level in the Huntsville City Schools, uses science as the driving force in the

overall curriculum. While her students studied the FOSS module
Wood, they also read about trees and animals that live in the forest
and discussed the work lumberjacks do. They even managed to
talk about Smoky the Bear and the importance of protecting trees
from forest fires.

But Patrick's all-time favorite experience with this module
came at the end of the year. She bubbles over with enthusiasm as
she describes how the module's final activity created a memorable
conclusion to her students' kindergarten days: "At the end of the
module, after studying different kinds of wood and their characteristics, the children applied what they had learned to make wood
sculptures. We showed them how to hammer, and they would still
be hammering if we hadn't gotten out of school. When all the
sculptures were completed, we invited parents and the rest of the
school to come see them. The fifth-graders complained that the
kindergarten children got to do all the fun stuff."

Yet in Patrick's school, older children have opportunities to
show off, too. After fourth-graders finish building their flashlights
during the STC *Electric Circuits* module, they come to the kindergarten class to show them how they work. In these ways, HASP has
fostered communication among the different grade levels in the
building.

The Struggle to Become Leaders
In addition to becoming proficient science teachers, HASP also ex-
pects the LMTs to become leaders in their own schools. Most
schools have two or three LMTs, from K–1, grades 2–3, and grades
4–6. While most teachers find leading their peers to be a challenge, Drummond and her fellow LMTs have discovered two
strategies that bring success—working closely with their principal
and planning carefully.

"Our principal was supportive, and she showed her support
by giving us faculty meeting time five or six times a year to give presentations on inquiry-centered science," says Drummond. "We
also made ourselves available during the year to answer the teachers' questions."

Yet even with this support, Drummond admits that "teaching
teachers is hard. . . . At first, the teachers didn't want to go through

the whole module. They thought that doing one or two activities was enough." With more experience, however, teachers have come to see that the way to build a concept is by working through the whole module. And by completing all the modules each year at each grade level, teachers help children gain a strong foundation in science.

Patrick had a less positive experience. "We encountered resistance from the teachers," she says. "I think that was partially because we came on too strong at first. We gave teachers too much information too fast. The result was overload, and a desire on the part of their teachers to go back to their rooms and shut the door."

To try to rectify the situation, Patrick and her colleagues backed off during the 1994-95 school year and decided not to initiate any faculty discussions, though Patrick did continue to answer questions and help with materials problems. This approach seemed to work better. By the end of the school year, more than 75 percent of the teachers were using the modules.

"We learn and go as we can," says Patrick. "It is clear that the program has made a big difference in children's attitudes about science."

Future Plans for HASP

In 1995, HASP received a Local Systemic Change Initiative (LSCI) grant from NSF. Under it, HASP will work with five additional school districts and build on the experience gained over the past two years. Participating school districts will select teachers and release them from their teaching responsibilities for a period of time so that they can work with the Institute for Science Education and train all the teachers in their districts. The program will further expand the number of school-based leaders.

While retaining successful components from the first grant, HASP has modified the program on the basis of the experiences of the past two years. For example, HASP learned that two years wasn't enough time to complete the needed reform. The LSCI will allow five years for professional development. Other realizations include the importance of cultivating teachers as leaders and the need to train principals so that they, too, can be advocates for the program.

"This is a rapidly changing field," says Wright. "We believe that HASP has demonstrated its utility, but it is a living model that improves through experience."

Lessons Learned

▶ A strong base of community support from local business and industry, local academic institutions, and the chamber of commerce can be extremely helpful.

▶ Teachers implementing reform activities need to be given administrative support. In many instances, principals may need training to help them understand the importance of identifying lead teachers who can collaborate with teachers new to inquiry-centered science.

▶ School districts should periodically revise their plans, incorporating the "lessons learned" into the program.

Pasadena, California

Pasadena Develops a Model for Teacher-Scientist Partnerships

The Pasadena Unified School District's 23 elementary schools (K–6) have 570 teachers and a student enrollment of 12,500. Forty-three percent of students are Hispanic/Latino, 35 percent are African American, and 17 percent are Euro-American. Inquiry-centered science is taught in both English and Spanish. Pasadena's science program is a joint effort of the Pasadena Unified School District and the California Institute of Technology. The program is based on the premise that scientists can contribute much to professional development activities for elementary school teachers.

The Pasadena Unified School District Science Program (formerly known as Project SEED) is the brainchild of Jerry Pine and Jim Bowers, scientists at the California Institute of Technology (CalTech). Pine is a physicist who has been active in elementary school science education reform since the 1960s; Bowers is a neurobiologist. In the mid-1980s, both men had children in the Pasadena schools. They knew that science education in the elementary schools could be better. On their own time, they began to visit exemplary elementary science programs such as the one established in Mesa, Arizona. Experience told them that a good deal of progress had already been made in elementary school science reform. They wanted to move forward; they didn't want to reinvent the wheel. So the two scientists formed an alliance with Michael Klentschy, then associate superintendent for instruction in the Pasadena Unified School District, and formulated a plan to introduce inquiry-centered science units into the district's elementary schools.

Scientists: The Heart of It All

The involvement of CalTech scientists is at the heart of Pasadena's science education program. At the beginning, the watchwords were "think small." They approached Klentschy and secured his enthusiastic endorsement. Having gotten the district's permission to begin a pilot program in one school, Bowers and Pine then met Jennifer Yuré, a science teacher at the Eugene Field Elementary School. During the next five years, Yuré recalls, they "just tried things out," as they sought to determine the best way to introduce teachers to hands-on science. "We finally came up with what we thought was the best model," she says. "It's teachers and scientists working together."

It's "working together" that makes the Pasadena program unique. Many programs use scientists as expert consultants; at Pasadena, scientists and teachers work side by side. Rather than lecture, the scientists work as co-facilitators with resource teachers as they train teachers in the use of the science modules that make up the program. The unique training model was supported by a five-year grant from the National Science Foundation.

CalTech's Leila Gonzalez first heard about the program from Bowers, then her professor, when she was a postdoctoral fellow in biology in 1989. The affinity was immediate. "Something inside me said, 'Yes. This is the way science should be taught,'" she recalls.

Today, she works for the program full-time as a liaison between the scientific and educational communities. The recruitment and training of scientists are her major responsibilities.

Recruitment, Gonzalez admits, is not a hurdle, given the degree of local support for the program. Volunteers include not only CalTech faculty but also students, alumni, retirees, and parents. Aware of the need for female role models in science, Gonzalez has made a special effort to recruit volunteers from organizations such as the American Association of University Women. About 150 scientists currently participate in the Pasadena program.

All new recruits undergo an orientation at CalTech. They become acquainted with the science kits and the structure of Pasadena's program. The inquiry-based learning process itself, however, needs no introduction. "This is the way you learn science as a graduate student," Gonzalez notes. After the orientation, they can also check out kits from the science materials center; in addition, program staff are always available for guidance.

Once the scientists are on board, their major responsibility is to participate in the teacher training programs. Approximately 10 teachers attend each of the day-long sessions, which are facilitated by a teacher-scientist team. The teachers break into small groups, and the scientist circulates informally among them. The scientists have two main responsibilities. One is to build the teachers' confidence and make them feel comfortable with the subject. "Our thrust is to support the teacher," Gonzalez emphasizes. "Science is a natural process, and you don't need to be a scientist to teach science." All 570 elementary school teachers in the district eventually underwent the training.

The other responsibility of the scientists is to model the scientific process. "Sometimes teachers have difficulty believing that involvement in the scientific process is more important than just knowing the facts," notes Yuré, who is now coordinator of the Pasadena Unified School District Science Program. "Teachers tell us that they have difficulty, for example, asking open-ended questions. Thus, we ask the scientist to model this process." Scientists also help the teachers keep the "big picture" in mind. Teachers learn to focus on the purpose of experiments and the connection between them rather than on the details.

After they've taught their first module, teachers return for a second training session. These sessions are again facilitated by a teacher-scientist team. At this point, qualms about classroom management have passed. Together, the groups discuss topics such as assessment of student learning or a particular activity within the unit.

It "Just Clicked"

In some cases, the teacher-scientist relationship goes further. A scientist may begin to visit the classroom of a teacher he or she met during a staff development session.

Such was the case with Barbara Bray, a third-grade lead teacher at the Field School, and scientist Josée Morissette, who is completing her doctorate at CalTech. They met, Morissette recalls, by "pure luck" as co-trainers of a module called *Clay Boats*. The relationship "just clicked." Bray emphasizes how easily Morissette has become a part of her classes. Before Morissette's visits, Bray recalls, the children had a "whole stereotypical view of what a scientist was and what they do. Josée changed that. The children feel comfortable having her in the room."

Exactly what happens when a teacher and a scientist get together? Each learns from the other, and learning horizons widen. "Barbara knows what third-graders will find appropriate," Morissette notes. "She's also open to brainstorming ideas about how to do things better." Having discovered, for example, that *Clay Boats* did not include student activities that involved liquids of different densities, Bray and Morissette decided to enrich the unit by adding activities that involved such liquids as glycerin, alcohol, vinegar, and oil. Moreover, the next time Bray presented the module at a staff development session, she included information on the activities that she and Morissette had jointly developed.

The advantages of the teamwork are obvious. Having a scientist in the classroom, Bray believes, strengthens curricular integration. "We can use science as a vehicle or catalyst for other things," she explains. Morissette points to shifts in student attitudes. Students seem more confident. They are more willing to try new things out, and they are more comfortable with "not always knowing the right answer," she believes.

Focusing on Assessment

Opportunities for growth remain, even for a mature program such as Pasadena's. One current focus of staff development activities is assessment.

Assessment study groups have been formed for each grade level. Members include a resource teacher from the Pasadena Unified School District Science Program, a scientist, and three teachers who have extensive experience with the kit for which assessments are being developed. Gail Baxter, a research investigator from the University of Michigan, is a consultant to this grant-supported program.

Assessments are needed for a variety of reasons. Some modules use traditional paper-and-pencil tests, which do not adequately reflect inquiry-based learning. In other cases, the teachers have enhanced the module, and active assessments are needed to document student performance in these new areas. Equally important, Gonzalez observes, is that "in creating an assessment, teachers really get a feel for what's important in the unit."

The study group meetings, Yuré explains, give teachers a chance to ask basic questions: What do we want the kids to learn? What are they learning? How are we teaching it? Morissette adds, "Once teachers get comfortable with the units, they don't necessarily focus on the scientific principles. Designing an assessment helps them get a grasp of the four or five key principles presented in a kit."

The study groups have found that embedded assessments (assessments that are woven into a class activity) are especially helpful, because they can give teachers feedback about student learning while the module is still in progress. This allows the teacher to modify the activities or teaching approach to meet learners' needs. All assessment instruments are pilot-tested in the classroom. Morissette, for example, has a key role both in the third-grade assessment study group and in testing the assessments in Bray's classroom.

Scientists are an integral part of the district's science program. They are present at the beginning, when new teachers open their first kits. They also continue to be involved as teachers become more skilled at teaching science, contributing their unique perspective to the development of performance-based assessment tools. "The scientists are unbelievably dedicated to making a difference in children's learning," says Bray. The program, she believes, is "not turning students into scientists; it's letting them learn in a vital new way. And it's a wonderful opportunity for teachers."

Lessons Learned

▶ Scientists and engineers can become involved in all phases of planning and implementing an inquiry-based elementary science program.

▶ Pairing teachers and scientists in the classroom can be a mutually satisfying learning experience. Such relationships, however, cannot be forced. They work best when they develop naturally over the course of working together.

▶ Teachers can benefit from the opportunity to work in small groups to develop assessment tools. Many teachers find that focusing on assessment enables them to better understand the scientific principles in a curriculum module.

San Francisco, California

A University Works Collaboratively with a City School District

*The San Francisco Unified School District serves approximately 35,000 elementary students in 75 elementary schools. Students come from urban and suburban neighborhoods across the economic spectrum. Eighty-five percent of San Francisco's students are minorities, including African American, Hispanic, and Asian. Thirty percent of the students come from families in which English is not the primary language.**

City Science is the story of a successful collaboration between the University of California at San Francisco (UCSF) and the San Francisco Unified School District. Between 1991 and 1995, City Science worked closely with the district and made significant contributions to the professional development of 100 teachers and the development of teacher-scientist relationships. Bruce Alberts, then a faculty member at UCSF and now president of the National Academy of Sciences, was instrumental in starting City Science.

The year was 1991. City Science, a project sponsored by the University of California at San Francisco (UCSF) in collaboration with the San Francisco Unified School District (SFUSD) through their Science and Health Education Partnership (SEP), had just received funding from the National Science Foundation (NSF) to implement a districtwide elementary science reform project.

City Science had developed a simple design for the program. Its goal was to expand the use of hands-on, inquiry-centered science teaching in the district by training a cadre of 100 lead teachers over four years. These teachers would be responsible for bringing the inquiry-centered approach to their schools. City Science also had secured funding to hire a full-time science resource teacher who would provide support to classroom teachers and be responsible for refurbishing the science kits.

But plans have a way of changing once the work actually begins. When City Science coordinators began implementing their program, other science education initiatives were already under way. In 1990, the California State Department of Education had published a radically different science framework, which stressed the importance of teaching the "big ideas" of science, such as energy and scale and structure. According to the district's adoption cycle, it was slated to align its curriculum with the California framework by 1992.

Another influence in the district was the program sponsored by School in the Exploratorium (SITE), a museum-based professional development effort. SITE had been training district teachers for more than a decade through intensive four-week institutes focusing on science inquiry. Finally, the school district had established the San Francisco Science Leadership Project, a three-year program designed to provide intensive training to 27 teachers who would be charged with the task of bringing inquiry-centered science to their schools and making key decisions about the science curriculum.

What proved to be the link among these program was the teachers, who worked together and discovered how their teaching could be strengthened by sharing ideas with their peers.

A Push for Professional Development

When City Science began work on the NSF project in 1991, its main vehicle for training was slated to be a kit-based curriculum program. Initially, the teachers were intimidated by the kits. "It was like going to the dentist to get the teachers to open the kits and get going," recalls Janice Low, former City Science director. "It's very scary to change your whole program overnight—to let the unknown into your classroom. Teachers wanted to improve their science teaching, but they had to be encouraged to use the new curriculum units."

City Science coordinators decided to proceed slowly. During the summer institute, the lead teachers used selected modules as a starting point to explore relevant science content, pedagogy, alternative assessment strategies, and leadership development. They received stipends and graduate credit for their involvement in the program.

At the end of the first summer institute, the teachers were given a full year to assimilate what they had learned and to prepare themselves to work with other teachers at their schools. Jan Tuomi, one of the program's founders, thinks that giving the lead teachers time to learn was a significant factor in the success of the program. The hiatus gave the participants an opportunity to practice what they had learned: to refine their teaching styles according to principles of inquiry-centered learning, to reflect on their classroom experiences, and to crystallize their own thinking about the instruction they had received. As a result, City Science alumni are now more effective and credible as coaches to their peers.

Over the subsequent three years of the program, City Science also discovered the importance of drawing on teachers from the city's other two major science reform initiatives. Science Leadership Project teachers served as mentor teachers for City Science summer institutes, and City Science teachers participated in workshops held at the Exploratorium. Graduates of the Exploratorium's programs also became involved in City Science and the Science Leadership Project. In these ways, the three separate programs became more united in their efforts and succeeded in training a large pool of teachers.

The Role of Scientists

Scientists had an integral role in the City Science program. After considering several approaches, the program initially opted to team each of six master teachers, one from each grade, with two UCSF scientists. During the first summer institute, the scientist-teacher teams introduced participants to inquiry-centered science modules. Over the subsequent three years, however, teachers worked with only one scientist.

The SEP executive director and City Science's co-principal investigator, Liesl Chatman, believes that scientists have much to gain from being part of such a partnership. "It's not a partnership if the scientists aren't learning," she says. "The scientists aren't just there to reform elementary science in the classroom—they're there to learn something themselves. . . . When the benefit is all the way around, the partnership becomes meaningful and sustainable."

Margaret Clark, SEP director and science coordinator for City Science, was among the first scientists who worked with teachers. She found the experience enlightening, giving her a "strong appreciation of teachers' teaching skills and an understanding of how to facilitate learning." Clark also found that "scientists are very good at making connections between major concepts and daily phenomena, which is very important in making science relevant to both teachers and students."

Teachers, too, found the partnership enormously beneficial. "Scientists put more credibility into what we were doing," says Denise Ebisuzaki, a third-grade teacher in San Francisco. "They were able to catch errors before we conveyed them to students. For example, in one module, scientists helped us understand that the teacher's guide had specified the wrong wire length to complete one experiment. A mistake like that could make or break a lesson."

Curriculum Adoption and Its Ramifications

In 1992, the district adopted module-based, inquiry-centered science curriculum materials for all 75 of the district's elementary schools. The materials support the core curriculum, which was developed in 1990. City Science and district teachers collaborated on the final choice of curriculum materials, which included modules from both the Full Option Science System and Insights. At this point, the district faced a new challenge: How could all of the elementary school teachers be prepared to begin teaching inquiry-centered science? Where would the district find the resources for this enormous undertaking?

To resolve these issues, the district asked City Science and its cadre of 100 lead teachers to join a smaller group of the SFUSD science leadership teachers and mentor teachers to become presenters, mentors, and leaders in efforts to introduce all of the district's teachers to inquiry-centered science. As part of this development effort, the district hired an outside consultant who showed the teachers how to organize workshops and gave them opportunities to practice on each other. "We told teachers that their experience with the modules was invaluable," says Low. "They know the day-to-day difficulties of working through the modules. Their experience gave them credibility with other teachers."

In the end, the teachers' hard work paid off. "I loved taking a leadership role and helping other teachers out," says Dan Brady, a third-grade teacher. "We were able to introduce the teachers to the modules in a structured way." Low concurs, noting that for the first time in the district's history, teachers were given six professional development days over two years, which enabled them to build a foundation for beginning to implement the modules. Low calls this move "unprecedented" and a "big risk" for the new superintendent, who made the final decision on the basis of his observation that a strong science program often meant that the school was operating at a high level. Through the training experience, City Science teachers grew as leaders, and the district teachers were better equipped to teach the science modules.

Materials Support

To further support the modular-based science program, SFUSD has established a central materials management center. It asks the schools to take more responsibility for their maintenance than other districts do, however. The system works like this: Each school in the district is issued four modules for every two teachers at each grade level. Generally, the kits contain enough consumable materials for two classes to use before a refurbishment request is sent back to the materials center. When the kits are ready for refurbishment, a lead teacher or an administrative staff member completes the necessary requisitions for the replacement materials. The materials are then sent back to the school, again with a sufficient quantity of supplies for two uses. The kits are kept at the schools, not at the materials management center.

Although the system has worked fairly well, some teachers point out that not all of the problems have been worked out of the materials aspect of the program. "The reordering process is time-consuming and burdensome," says Brady. "I think it would be easier if the district created a new order form, where we could check off what we needed instead of having to write it in. In my view, the materials component is critical: without the supplies, teachers won't use the modules."

Future Plans

In 1995, the UCSF and SFUSD received a five-year Local Systemic Change Initiative grant from the NSF to continue and greatly expand the City Science effort. The new grant will support the strengthening of leadership from within the district. One of City Science's most important contributions to science education reform was realizing that the district—not outside consultants— must take the lead. "Establishing an appropriate leadership structure is key," says Chatman. "The district must come first."

The new grant will also strive to bring more teachers into the program and to raise the level of inquiry-centered instruction by those already using the modules. It also includes an important new feature—eight focus schools designed to become models for science education reform at the school level. Planners have to involve the whole neighborhood in the effort, including parents, businesses, and other local resources.

City Science teachers and staff are looking forward to continuing the work begun over the past four years. As she prepares to embark on the second phase, Clark reflects on the program's progress to date. "Science education reform is never really 'finished,'" she says. "Progress is ongoing. The real issue is to leap from working with a small, committed group of teachers to going districtwide. It's difficult to communicate with and motivate other teachers outside the small group. It's a huge leap, and we're just at the beginning of that task."

Lessons Learned

▶ Although partnerships are an effective way to bring about change in science education, the outside organization must learn how to collaborate with the school district. Reform will be most significant when the district assumes a strong leadership role.

▶ Professional development is crucial, because it provides teachers with the support they need to teach inquiry-centered science effectively. Furthermore, teachers need time and additional training if they are to become leaders of science education reform at the district level.

▶ Forming partnerships between scientists and teachers can add an important dimension to the district's professional development program.

Green Bay, Wisconsin

The Einstein Project Builds a Science Program Through Community Partnerships

A nonprofit corporation founded in 1991, the Einstein Project is a business and community partnership that supports high-quality science, math, and technology education in nine public school districts, the Green Bay Catholic Diocese, and the Oneida Nation's Schools in northeastern Wisconsin. Over the past three years, the project has served 75 schools, 1,900 teachers, and 25,000 elementary school students.

The program is founded on the belief that a long-term commitment, volunteerism, and a few generous funders can get a science program off the ground. The program's founders developed some innovative strategies for procuring funds that other programs may want to consider using.

The Einstein Project did not have any support when it started—no funding, no appropriate curriculum materials, no professional development program. What propelled the project forward, according to Cecilia Turriff, one of its founders, was "a vision." Having taught all her life, Turriff says that everywhere she went, she saw a tremendous need for both good science materials and expertise in the teaching of science. "I knew I was doing the wrong thing," she says, "but I didn't know what was right."

Along with her scientist husband, David, Turriff assembled a group of Green Bay public school teachers who were concerned about the lack of high-quality science education in the area and arranged a meeting with Foth and Van Dyke, a large architectural and engineering firm headquartered in Green Bay. From that meeting evolved what was to be the essence of the Einstein Project: business and education communities brought together in a cooperative effort. The project soon spread to all the private and public school systems of Brown County, Wisconsin, including the Catholic Diocese. Early on, it became clear that, except for the Green Bay school system, no single school or business in the area was large enough to support a substantial partnership. By banding together, however, financial and human resources could be pooled that could make a difference in the educational process.

David Ewald, district administrator of the Denmark, Wisconsin, Public Schools and board president of the Einstein Project, says that when he thinks back to that time, "I don't picture superintendents around the table. I think of business people and teachers around the table." He attributes the project's initial success to this core group of founders, their "strong, energetic leadership up front who believed in an almost evangelistic sense that hands-on, inquiry-centered science was the right thing."

Solidifying the Partnership

In May 1991, a board of directors was appointed with a representative from each public school system, the Catholic Diocese, each of the three institutions of higher education in the county, six local businesses, and the Cooperative Educational Service Agency No. 7, the liaison agency between the school districts and the state superintendent's office. Accommodation in the by-laws of incorporation was made for up to 12 business representatives to serve on the board. One of the first acts of the project's board of directors was to apply to the Internal Revenue Service for 501(c)(3) status. This designation enables the Einstein Project to receive federal and state grants as well as tax-deductible charitable donations from businesses and individuals.

In the first year of operation, the Einstein Project applied for over one-half million dollars of state and federal grant money and carried out a capital fund drive in the business community for $450,000. Even before the official fund-raising campaign was launched, several businesses began supporting the project. Wisconsin Public Service, headquartered in Green Bay, made a substantial contribution of time, materials, and money. Paper Converting, Inc., also in Green Bay, made a donation that allowed the implementation of programs to get under way. The Wisconsin Department of Public Instruction awarded the Einstein Project a grant from its Science, Mathematics, and Technology Grant Program to be used for operational expenses, and the American Chemical Society awarded the project one of six national grants to assist in the development of science partnerships.

Why were businesses and organizations willing to contribute time, talent, and funds to support the Einstein Project? Many of these founders and supporters seemed to understand that tomorrow's problem solvers are sitting in today's classrooms. For example, Dan Bollom, president and chief executive officer of Wisconsin Public Service, says, "I've always been a strong proponent of education. As a businessman and school board member, I feel there is so much we can do to help students be better prepared for the future. The Einstein Project will enable students to see the many possibilities awaiting them in the world of science and technology."

One of the project's first activities was to test two nationally known hands-on science programs—Full Option Science System (FOSS) and Science and Technology for Children (STC)—at 10 schools. After evaluating these pilot tests, the project's leaders decided to purchase, maintain, and distribute STC kits to participating schools from a centralized resource center. In 1992 and 1993, the project purchased between 100 and 150 kits. By 1994, the number of kits was close to 300, and they were serving between 12,000 and 15,000 students. Each school pays a $100 rental fee each time it uses a science kit. In 1995, the project expanded to include FOSS's kindergarten materials. The goal for the coming school year is to serve between 25,000 and 30,000 schoolchildren.

Teacher volunteers do the in-service training required before kits can be rented. Diane McNeill, currently a science teacher at Edison Middle School in Green Bay, was one of the first teachers to pilot-test the kits for the Einstein Project, and she has been training teachers in their use ever since. McNeill says, "I have done training at all of the summer academies [annual, week-long teacher enhancement workshops aimed at science and math] as well as after school and on Saturdays, all on my own time. When I ask myself why, the answer is the kids. They're benefiting so much—and I want to help other teachers who want to become involved. I don't want them to lose their enthusiasm." She adds that inquiry-based science teaching has benefited her personally, as well. "It has improved all of my teaching skills. I can relate using the inquiry-based method to many other subjects."

"Door Knocking" Produces Results

As Ewald says, there was a lot of "knocking on doors," especially in the early days. As one of the main "door knockers," Cecilia Turriff found herself spreading the word of the project's mission to anyone who seemed the slightest bit interested. She went to local school boards, PTA and Girl Scout meetings, meetings of the chamber of commerce, and business conventions. "My job was to finagle," says Turriff, "and I did it well."

If businesses didn't have funds to donate, the project asked for free materials—or materials at a discount—for the kits. The requests were met with a variety of contributions. One business donated plant stands for the *Plant Growth and Development* unit. One hundred buckets for use in the *Chemical Tests* units came free from a plastics company in California. In addition to providing seed money for project development and needs assessment, Wisconsin Public Service funded the restocking of the *Electric Circuits* unit. When the project's photocopying machine went on the blink, Turriff called a company in Milwaukee that serviced the machine at a saving of about $600. (She says the machine is clunking along to this day.) Finally, having identified the original manufacturers of some key items in the STC science kits, the project was able to go directly to the supply source itself. Motors for the *Magnets and Motors* unit, which previously had cost $1.27 apiece, were obtained for a mere 20 cents apiece, for example. Turriff estimates that between January and April of 1994, she helped save the project more than $30,000 in supplies by getting them donated or at reduced costs.

Even a building was, in a sense, donated by the community. In 1991, the Einstein Project occupied a house located on the grounds of a local parochial school. This house was—and still is—rented to the project for $1 per year in exchange for the project using the school as a place to develop programs. Originally used as the project's science resource center, today that building houses the Einstein Project's four-person full-time staff.

Volunteers Are Key

In addition to the teachers who volunteer to do the training, an enormous number of other volunteers augment the project's small staff. These dedicated individuals put in hundreds of hours in the 3,000-plus-square-foot warehouse space that currently serves as the resource center. Volunteers stock the new kits, refurbish the old ones, and prepare the bags of materials that go into the kits. According to Project Director Jim Cornell, many of the volunteers are senior citizens, "doctors, dentists, teachers, and people who just care enough to give their time." For example, a retired carpenter came in and built an enormous stand on which to grow plants. A retired dentist made balances for the *Balancing and Weighing* unit.

The extensive use of volunteers also makes the project attractive to funders. As Cornell explains, "It makes the project very attractive to people who want to support it financially. They know that very little of their money goes into overhead."

Anna Kim, a former clerk in the resource center, says, "A volunteer network can play a big part in keeping a science resource center together. Without this kind of community support, it would have been a struggle to make it work." And the volunteers seem to get a lot out of their experience. According to Kim, "They really enjoy it. They feel like they are doing something useful. In time, they came to feel like family—second moms and dads."

Looking to the Future

What does the future have in store for the Einstein Project? One of the current priorities is to strengthen the use of computer technology. The project has established a countywide bulletin board system, complete with electronic mail, conferences in each major science discipline, and CD-ROM capability. Students, teachers, scientists, and myriad project stakeholders may access the bulletin board system with a local phone call from a modem-equipped computer. On-line conferences, which are intended to broaden users' knowledge base within a specific science discipline, are serviced by one or more experts from the community. For example, professionals from Green Bay's two largest hospitals service the medical conference, local veterinarians tend the vet conference, and a high school biology class researches questions posed by elementary school children in a life sciences conference. In effect, the technology component provides a forum where individuals can sign on electronically and talk to each other on-line, leave messages, read other people's questions and answers, and establish a dialogue with an expert.

In addition, the project is working with teachers to identify science modules that lend themselves to collecting and graphing data. The project plans to facilitate the recording of the data on computer spreadsheets or databases so that the data can be reproduced readily in text or graphic formats. This integration of technology with scientific discovery will give students a better understanding of how computers are used in business, industry, medicine, and other fields.

The project also continues to confront financial realities. According to Cornell, "Our ultimate goal is that the project will be nearly self-sustaining, relying very little on repetitive cash contributions from local businesses and individuals." But Cornell is quick to acknowledge the essential role the business community has played in the project's growth. He says, "Without the belief and commitment from this key segment of the community, the project could not have moved from concept to reality. Their generous contributions of time, expertise, and funds have rendered this a total community effort, one that has a very high probability of continued long-term success."

Lessons Learned

▶ Enlisting local business and community support has many benefits. Businesses can donate funds, but they are also a potential source of materials, technical expertise, and guidance in the business world.

▶ The program has benefited from a broad funding base that includes a combination of federal and state grants, as well as contributions and in-kind services from local businesses.

▶ It is important to involve teachers in inquiry-centered programs every step of the way. Teachers can help with program research and development and in-service training, and they can serve as proponents of the program.

▶ An efficient, well-stocked materials center is essential and can be kept running smoothly with the help of community volunteers.

Epilogue

Nothing is in the mind that is not first in the hand.
— **Aristotle, 384–322 B.C.**

For more than a decade, the National Science Resources Center (NSRC) has been actively engaged in elementary science education reform. During that time, we have been fortunate to develop meaningful partnerships with more than 200 school districts. From these partnerships have emerged a few "basic truths" about reform. Districts new to this work may find that these truths become guideposts as they set out to bring inquiry-centered science to their elementary schools.

▶ Close partnerships between the stakeholders involved in science education reform are preferable to the distant relations that were previously the norm.

▶ Leaders in science education reform must work in teams characterized by concern about elementary science education, consistency in the way they implement change, and commitment to seeing the program through to completion.

▶ Strategic planning serves as the umbrella for all the elements of reform. It gives stakeholders a clear idea of where to go and the key things that must be done to get there. This information establishes how each individual's efforts fit the goals and provides a standard against which to measure how well the goals are being achieved.

▶ It is not enough to design a good curriculum; the processes needed to implement that curriculum must be designed at the same time.

▶ It is crucial for districts to begin with some concrete initiatives and to demonstrate some successful results, even if they are small.

▶ Teachers must be provided with the materials needed to teach inquiry-centered science. Furthermore, leaders must be provided with opportunities for continuous professional development.

The publication of the *National Science Education Standards* has given new direction to the elementary science education reform movement of the 1980s and 1990s. For the first time, school districts engaged in reform have clear-cut goals. The *Standards* delineates what children should know and be able to do in science from kindergarten through high school. The NSRC model for reform provides guidance on how to achieve these goals. Of particular importance is the development of a shared vision of teaching science through inquiry and the adoption of an implementation strategy that focuses on the five key elements of reform—curriculum design, professional development, science materials support, assessment, and administrative and community support.

Informed by the *Standards* and enlightened through experience, we are ready to embark on the next decade of reform. New issues have emerged, and we are faced with new challenges. For example, although the NSRC and other organizations have reached several hundred school districts, our goal is to increase these numbers significantly so that the majority of the nation's children have an opportunity to learn science through inquiry. We must also work to improve the quality of inquiry-centered science in districts that have already institutionalized reform.

Charles Hardy
Deputy Director
National Science Resources Center

Notes

Chapter 1

1. National Research Council, *National Science Education Standards* (Washington, D.C.: National Academy Press, 1996), p. 23.
2. H. J. Hausman, *Choosing a Science Program for the Elementary School* (Washington, D.C.: Council for Basic Education, Occasional Papers No. 24, 1972), p. 5.
3. Excerpted from the keynote address given by Philip and Phylis Morrison at the Summer 1989 National Science Resources Center's Elementary Science Leadership Institute.
4. J. Elstgeest, "Teaching Science by Posing Problems," *Prospects* 8, no. 1 (1970): 2.
5. K. R. Mechling and D. L. Oliver, *Handbook IV: What Research Says About Elementary Science* (Washington, D.C.: National Science Teachers Association, 1983), p. 8.
6. American Association for the Advancement of Science, *Benchmarks for Science Literacy* (New York: Oxford University Press, 1993), p. 4.
7. National Research Council, *Standards*, p. 20.
8. Elstgeest, "Teaching Science by Posing Problems," p. 2.
9. H. Gardner, *The Unschooled Mind: How Children Think and How Schools Should Teach* (New York: BasicBooks, 1993), p. 13.
10. L. B. Resnick, *Education and Learning to Think* (Washington, D.C.: National Academy Press, 1987), p. 47.
11. Ibid, pp. 35-36.
12. A. J. Reynolds, T. Hoffer, and J. D. Miller, "Investigating the Effects of Inquiry-Based Elementary Science Programs," paper presented at the 1991 annual meeting of the American Association for the Advancement of Science, Washington, D.C.
13. T. Bredderman, "Activity Science—The Evidence Shows It Matters," *Science and Children* 20 (September 1982): 39-41.

Chapter 2

1. Piaget's seminal work, published in 1926, is *The Language and Thought of the Child* (London: Routledge). *The Psychology of the Child*, written with B. Inhelder, provides a good introduction to Piaget's ideas (New York: BasicBooks, 1969).

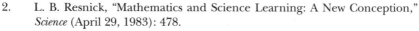

2. L. B. Resnick, "Mathematics and Science Learning: A New Conception," *Science* (April 29, 1983): 478.

3. Among the researchers who believed in a combination of "discovery" learning and traditional instruction was Jerome Bruner. His pivotal work is *Studies in Cognitive Growth,* by J. Bruner and M. J. Kenny (New York: John Wiley, 1965). David Ausubel, an educational psychologist, also espoused this view. His pivotal work is *Educational Psychology: A Cognitive View,* by D. P. Ausubel et al. (New York: Holt, Rinehart, and Winston, 1978).

4. L. F. Lowery, *The Biological Basis of Thinking and Learning* (Berkeley: University of California, 1992), p. 5.

5. J. M. Healy, *Endangered Minds: Why Our Children Don't Think* (New York: Simon & Schuster, 1990), pp. 72-73.

6. H. Gardner, *The Unschooled Mind* (New York: BasicBooks, 1991), p. 5.

7. Resnick, *Mathematics and Science Learning,* pp. 477-78.

8. This example is from an article by Bruce Watson and Richard Konicke: "Teaching for Conceptual Change: Confronting Children's Experience," *Phi Delta Kappa* (May 1990): 683-85.

9. S. Sprague, "Beyond Explicit Standards for Science Education," in *Redesigning the Science Curriculum,* R. W. Bybee and J. D. McInerney, eds. (Colorado Springs: BSCS, 1995), p. 92.

10. Resnick, *Mathematics and Science Learning,* pp. 477-78.

11. See Lowery, *The Biological Basis of Thinking and Learning,* for a more detailed discussion of this model.

Chapter 3

1. National Research Council, *National Science Education Standards* (Washington, D.C.: National Academy Press, 1996), p. 33.

Chapter 4

1. R. Evans, "The Human Face of Reform," *Educational Leadership* 51 (September 1993): 19.

2. S. M. Hord, W. L. Rutherford, L. Huling-Austin, and G. E. Hall, *Taking Charge of Change* (Alexandria, Va.: Association of Supervision and Curriculum Development, 1987).

3. W. Bennis and B. Nanus, *Leaders: The Strategies for Taking Charge* (New York: HarperPerennial, 1985), p. 28.

Chapter 5

1. National Research Council, *National Science Education Standards* (Washington, D.C.: National Academy Press, 1996), p. 23.

Chapter 6

1. The Regional Laboratory for Educational Improvement of the Northeast

and Islands, *Continuing to Learn: A Guidebook for Teacher Development* (Andover, Mass.: Regional Laboratory for Educational Improvement of the Northeast and Islands, 1987), p. 13.

2. National Research Council, *National Science Education Standards* (Washington, D.C.: National Academy Press, 1996), p. 58.

3. Research by D. C. Berliner found that teachers can fit into the following five categories: novice, advanced beginner, competent, proficient, and expert ("In Pursuit of the Expert Pedagogue," *Educational Researcher* 15, no. 9 (1986): 5-13). In this chapter, we focus on three of these categories: novice, competent, and expert.

4. National Research Council, *Standards*, p. 33.

Chapter 7

1. G. Hein, C. Baldassari, and L. Hudson, "Developing Inquiry-Centered Elementary School Science: Community Elementary Science Reform after Attendance at Summer Leadership Institutes 1989-1994, Third Year Evaluation Report" (Cambridge, Mass.: Lesley College, 1995), pp. 49-50.

2. This quote is from an unpublished white paper by Larry Small, former science supervisor for Schaumburg, Illinois, "Science Materials Support," 1992, p. 1.

Chapter 8

1. National Research Council, *National Science Education Standards* (Washington, D.C.: National Academy Press, 1996), pp. 76, 82.

Chapter 9

1. National Science Resources Center, "Corporate America's Impact on Elementary Science Education" (Washington, D.C.: National Science Resources Center, 1994), p. 5.

Appendix A

Professional Associations and U.S. Government Organizations

The following associations and government organizations are involved in science education reform and offer assistance relevant to elementary science teaching.

American Association for the Advancement of Science (AAAS), 1333 H St., N.W., Washington, DC 20005; (202) 326-6400.

The largest general scientific organization in the country and the largest federation of scientific societies in the world, with nearly 300 affiliated science societies and organizations. Programs sponsored by the AAAS Directorate for Education and Human Resources include the Annual Forum for School Science; Collaboration for Equity in Science; radio programs "Science Update" and "Kinetic City Super Crew" (the latter with teacher's guide, home activities, and call-in); and project SLIC (Science Linkages in the Community) to train people to teach science. Books in many fields of science and science education, including *IDEAAAS: Sourcebook for Science, Mathematics and Technology Education* (3rd ed.), and the newsletter *Science Education News*.

Project 2061, a long-term science education reform initiative for grades K–12, offers the following publications: *Science for All Americans,* on scientific literacy; *Benchmarks for Science Literacy,* a curriculum design tool defining expectations for science knowledge for grades 2, 5, 8, and 12; and other books and computer-based materials on curriculum design, exemplary resources, and research.

American Chemical Society, 1155 16th St., N.W., Washington, DC 20036; (202) 872-4600.

Principal professional society of chemists, with 145,000 members. Operation Chemistry (OpChem), funded by the National Science Foundation, sponsors two-week workshops for teacher-training teams and subsequent workshops nationwide for thousands of teachers. Offers Community Science Grants for children and adults to explore hands-on science as teams. Publishes curriculum guidelines, supplemental activities, audiovisual materials, and *WonderScience* (activities magazine for upper-elementary students and adults working together, published jointly with the American Institute of Physics); produces videos and booklets supporting chemists who go into the classroom, a newsletter, and posters.

American Geological Institute, 4220 King St., Alexandria, VA 22302; (703) 379-2480.

Federation of more than 25 professional, scientific, and technical associations in the earth sciences. Publications include *Adventures in Geology,* a text-based approach to geology and science teaching for grades K–3 and 4–6; and *Earth Science Content Guidelines,* a report, with activities, to guide the inclusion of earth science content in the K–12 curriculum. Publications include ideas and activities in the areas of solid earth, water, air, ice, life, and earth in space.

American Indian Science and Engineering Society, 1630 30th St., Suite 301, Boulder, CO 80301; (303) 492-8658.

Society of American Indian and non-Indian students, scientific professionals, and interested corporations that provides programs for American Indian students and their teachers to enhance student interest and abilities in science. Works to link hands-on, student-centered science to culture and community with uniquely Indian programs and curricula; science focus on biology, human biology, environmental sciences, and science/technology and society. Programs include workshops at society meetings, technical assistance, information hotline, and National American Indian

Science Fair. Publications include curriculum units, teacher's guides, audiovisual and computer-based materials, *Winds of Change Magazine* for students, and a newsletter.

American Institute of Physics, American Center for Physics, One Physics Ellipse, College Park, MD 20740-3843; (301) 209-3100.

Organization of 10 professional societies (totaling 75,000 members) and 19 affiliated societies in physics and related fields; concerned with collecting and disseminating information about physics, physics education, and the history of physics. Publications include *Physics Education News,* a semimonthly electronic newsletter, and *WonderScience,* an activities magazine for upper-elementary students and adults working together. *WonderScience* is published jointly with the American Chemical Society.

American Meteorological Society, 1701 K St., N.W., Suite 300, Washington, DC 20006; (202) 466-5728.

Professional scientific society of more than 11,000 members; focused on meteorology, climatology, and oceanography. Programs include two national projects—Project ATMOSPHERE (meteorology and climatology) and the newer Maury Project (oceanography)—to train K–12 teachers in these areas. Training includes one-week institutes for master teachers and monitoring of subsequent workshops nationwide in which the master teachers train other teachers. Publications include teacher's guides, materials, hands-on activities solely for use in the two projects; audiovisual and computer-based materials; and a newsletter.

American Physical Society, American Center for Physics, One Physics Ellipse, College Park, MD 20740; (301) 209-3200.

Principal professional society for physicists and physics students, with more than 40,000 members; focused primarily on physics and on physics education. Its Teacher-Scientist Alliance, a national cooperative effort operated with the American Association of Physics Teachers, is designed to mobilize scientists in support of efforts aimed at systemic reform of elementary science education. Scientists from areas with school districts engaged in systemic reform are recruited, taught about reform issues, and expected to recruit and teach other scientists in their areas.

The Annenberg/CPB Math and Science Project, 901 E St., N.W., Washington, DC 20004; (202) 879-9600.

A project working in partnership with education, policy, and civic organizations to promote reform in math and science education. Funds a wide range of programs, including Project PRISM, an extensive community outreach campaign conducted and coordinated by the National Urban League; Science Images, a series of videocassettes focusing on eight elementary and middle school teachers teaching a specific science concept, produced in collaboration with the North Central Regional Educational Laboratory; Private Universe Teacher Workshops, a series of videocassettes demonstrating how students' preconceived ideas can create barriers to learning, produced in collaboration with Harvard-Smithsonian Center for Astrophysics; and The Synergy Project, a series of videocassettes on the information needed for a strategic workshop for senior-level policymakers and educational administrators, produced in collaboration with the Education Commission of the States. Each videocassette program comes with print materials, such as a source book, fact sheets, a viewer's guide, or a workshop guide.

Association for Supervision and Curriculum Development (ASCD), 1250 N. Pitt St., Alexandria, VA 22314-1403; (703) 549-9110.

Educational association with more than 190,000 members. Disseminates information on educational research and practice and conducts professional development institutes of one to three days in major U.S. cities. Publications include *ASCD Curriculum Handbook, Brown's Directories of Instructional Programs* (annual guide to commercial materials), *Only the Best* (annual guide to computer-based materials), *Curriculum Materials Directory* (annual guide to noncommercial materials), *Educational Leadership* (journal), ASCD books, and *Hands-On Elementary Science* (materials for 20 workshops).

Association of Science Materials Centers, c/o Science and Social Sciences Resource Specialist, Mesa Public Schools, 143 South Alma School Rd., Mesa, AZ 85120-1096; (602) 898-7815.

Organization whose membership is made up of managers of districtwide or multidistrict science materials support centers. Provides information and technical assistance on how to establish and sustain a central science materials support center.

Association of Science-Technology Centers (ASTC), 1025 Vermont Ave., N.W., Suite 500, Washington, DC 20005; (202) 783-7200.

Worldwide organization of science centers and museums, planetariums, space theaters, nature centers, aquariums, natural history museums, children's museums, and other facilities, with more than 270 members in the United States and Canada. Created and operates YouthALIVE, a program for underserved adolescents (grades 5–12) delivered by nearly 50 museums that are members of either ASTC or the Association of Youth Museums. Newsletter, directory of programs, and "how-to" manual are available. The program provides hands-on enrichment programs with structured opportunities for grades 5–8, such as clubs, camps, classes, workshops, and field trips, to heighten interest and involvement of targeted adolescents in the physical sciences. Museums design their own programs, often working with community-based organizations, and seek minimum involvement of 120 hours per year for two or three years for each student. ASTC provides technical assistance and professional development for museum staff members.

Biological Sciences Curriculum Study (BSCS), Pikes Peak Research Park, 5415 Mark Dabling Blvd., Colorado Springs, CO 80918-3842; (719) 531-5550.

Organization dedicated to leadership in science education through the design, development, and implementation of curriculum materials. Extensive programs and publications, including curriculum materials for K–12, publications on science education reform, and a newsletter.

Council for Elementary Science International (CESI), c/o Dr. Betty Burchett, CESI Membership Chair, 212 Townsend Hall, University of Missouri, Columbia, MO 65211; (314) 882-4831.

Professional organization with 1,600 members and a Division Affiliate of the National Science Teachers Association, dedicated to stimulating, improving, and coordinating science teaching (grades pre-K–8). Publications include source books for teaching elementary science, research monographs on teaching science, and file sheets.

Council of State Science Supervisors, c/o Dr. Thomas Keller, Council President, Maine Department of Education, 23 State House Station, Augusta, ME 04333-0023; (207) 287-5920.

Organization consisting of a science supervisor/specialist/consultant from each of the 50 states, the District of Columbia, Puerto Rico, and Guam. Coordinates members' work in creating curriculum guidelines, frameworks, and standards within their respective areas, as well as information dissemination efforts.

Education Development Center, 55 Chapel St., Newton, MA 02160; (619) 969-7100.

International education research and development organization founded in 1958, with a Center for Learning, Teaching, and Technology among its subdivisions. Publications include *Insights,* a comprehensive K–6 science curriculum. Provides technical assistance to Statewide Systemic Initiatives in 24 states and Puerto Rico and assists several school districts in implementing systemic reform.

Educational Equity Concepts, 114 E. 32nd St., Suite 701, New York, NY 10016; (212) 725-1803.

National organization dedicated to producing educational programs and materials free from bias concerning gender, race and ethnicity, and disability and income. Organization has developed a physical science activity program (for pre-K–3), with hands-on curriculum materials, audiovisual materials, and facilitator notebook. Staff development and parent training are provided. Also has developed a physical science curriculum (for grades K–2 or K–3), a curriculum guide, and a staff development guide.

Eisenhower National Clearinghouse for Mathematics and Science Education, The Ohio State University, 1929 Kenny Rd., Columbus, OH 43210-1079; (614) 292-7784.

Funded through the U.S. Department of Education and administered by the Ohio State University, the Clearinghouse aims to provide K–12 teachers with a central source of information on science and mathematics curriculum materials. Maintains a comprehensive collection of curriculum resources in many formats—print, audio, multimedia, video, kits, and games. Publishes a detailed catalog, *ENC Online*, available via modem (1-800-362-4448), Telnet and Gopher (enc.org), and World Wide Web (http://www.enc.org). Many other products and services are available in print and electronic format, including a database of federal programs, electronic visits to particular schools, and a reference service. Information is also available via e-mail (info@enc.org).

ERIC Clearinghouse for Science, Mathematics, and Environmental Education, The Ohio State University, 1929 Kenny Rd., Columbus, OH 43210-1080; (614) 292-6717, (800) 276-0462, (800) LET-ERIC (for new users).

Clearinghouse and international information network, 1 of 16 in the ERIC (Educational Resources Information Center) system, which is supported by the U.S. Department of Education. ERIC collects, catalogs, and provides access to educational materials; offers reference and referral services; produces bibliographic information; and maintains an extensive database of reports, curricular and instructional materials, evaluations, and information on programs, practices, and policies in science, mathematics, and environmental education. Accessible and searchable on CD-ROM or over the Internet, through e-mail (ericse@osu.edu), Gopher (gopher.ericse.ohio-state.edu), and the World Wide Web (http://www.ericse.ohio-state.edu).

Geological Society of America, P.O. Box 9140, Boulder, CO 80301-9140; (303) 447-2020.

Professional scientific society with more than 16,000 members. Sponsors Partners for Excellence Program (PEP), a national network of people committed to enhancing science education for children and fostering collaborations and partnerships between teachers and scientists. Offers sessions for teachers at the annual meeting and free PEP membership for teachers. Programs managed by PEP include a national database of scientist partners (for grades K–12), scientist mentors, and tours for students of the society's facility.

High-Scope Educational Foundation, 600 N. River St., Ypsilanti, MI 48198-2898; (313) 485-2000.

Research, development, training, and public advocacy organization focused on bringing inquiry-centered science to grades K–3. Conducts K–3 workshop sessions at meetings and week-long K–3 science workshops. Produces a teacher's manual that includes K–3 student activities.

Institute for Chemical Education, University of Wisconsin, Department of Chemistry, 1101 University Ave., Madison, WI 53706; (608) 262-3033.

National organization based at the University of Wisconsin at Madison, with a network of field centers and affiliates across the country devoted to helping teachers at all grade levels (kindergarten through college) revitalize science education. Offers two-week workshops at various regional sites, four-week workshops in Madison, summer fellowships, and Chem Camps for students (grades 5–8). Publishes instructional materials for teachers, kits, and a newsletter.

Lawrence Hall of Science, University of California, Centennial Dr., Berkeley, CA 94720; (510) 642-5132.

Science center involved in research in science and mathematics education, teacher training, and curriculum development. Extensive programs and publications, including two curriculum projects—Great Explorations in Math and Science and the Full Option Science System.

National Association for Research in Science Teaching (NARST), c/o Dr. John R. Staver, NARST Executive Secretary, Center for Science Education, 219 Bluemont Hall, Kansas State University, Manhattan, KS 66506; (913) 532-6294.

Professional association of more than 1,000 members worldwide designed to improve science teaching through research. Holds an annual convention with more than 200 research papers. Publications include *Journal of Research in Science Teaching* and a newsletter.

National Association for the Education of Young Children, 1509 16th St., N.W., Washington, DC 20036; (800) 424-2460.

Association of 75,000 professional educators and others involved in preschool and primary school education. Publishes more than 100 books, monographs, and other materials (catalog available) on early childhood education and the journal *Young Children.*

National Association of Biology Teachers, 11250 Roger Bacon Dr., No. 19, Reston, VA 22090-5202; (703) 471-1134.

Professional society of more than 7,000 biology educators and administrators representing all grade levels. Offers teacher training and professional development, builds alliances between scientists and teachers, promotes hands-on investigative biology, and develops curriculum and science policy. Publications include monographs and special publications, *The American Biology Teacher* (magazine), a newsletter, and a catalog of materials.

National Association of Elementary School Principals, 1615 Duke St., Alexandria, VA 22314; (703) 684-3345.

Organization serving 26,000 elementary and middle school principals in the United States and Canada, with an affiliate in every state. Publishes the *Principal* (a magazine), a newsletter, and other publications.

National Center for Improving Science Education, 2000 L St., N.W., Suite 603, Washington, DC 20036; (202) 467-0652.

Division of The NETWORK, Inc., of Andover, Massachusetts, an organization dedicated to science education reform. Provides guidance for educational policymakers, curriculum developers, and practitioners by synthesizing findings in policy studies, research reports, and exemplary practices and by transforming them into practical resources, with one subject area selected each year. Offers workshops by technical assistance teams. Publications include curriculum guidelines, guidelines for policymakers, information for parents, books, and monographs.

National Center for Research on Teacher Learning, Michigan State University, College of Education, 116 Erickson Hall, East Lansing, MI 48824-1034; (514) 355-9302.

Research center supported by the U.S. Department of Education. Conducts research on how teachers learn to teach and engage students in active learning, with some projects specifically focused on science and mathematics.

National Center for Science Teaching and Learning, The Ohio State University, 1929 Kenny Rd., Columbus, OH 43210-1015; (614) 292-3339.

Research center supported by the U.S. Department of Education. Conducts research on noncurricular factors, such as organizational and technological issues, that affect science students and teachers (grades K–12).

National Network for Science and Technology, 6H Berkey Hall, Michigan State University, East Lansing, MI 48824-1111; (517) 355-0180.

Network of land-grant universities, Cooperative Extension Systems, and other organizations in all 50 states concerned with children, youth, and families at risk. Promotes science and technology literacy. Services include technical and program assistance for extension faculty and collaborators to develop and implement effective programs, national and regional training, research and development, and maintenance of an electronic clearinghouse. For further information, contact by e-mail (nnst@mes.umn.edu) or Gopher and Telnet (gopher-cyfernet.mes.umn.edu).

National PTA—National Congress of Parents and Teachers, 330 N. Wabash St., Suite 2100, Chicago, IL 60611-3604; (312) 670-6782.

Organization dedicated to bringing parents, teachers, students, principals, and administrators together with the goal of involving the community in school activities. Works on child advocacy legislation through the Office of Governmental Relations in Washington, D.C. Publications include *Looking in on Your School: A Workbook for Improving Public Education, National PTA Directory* (quarterly), *PTA Handbook, PTA Today, What's Happening in Washington* (bimonthly), and a newsletter.

National Research Council (NRC), Center for Science, Mathematics, and Engineering Education, 2101 Constitution Ave., Washington, DC 20418; (202) 334-2353.

NRC is the operating arm of three honorary academies: the National Academy of Sciences, the National Academy of Engineering, and the Institute of Medicine. NRC's primary function is advising the federal government on science and technology policy. It has become increasingly active in efforts to improve science education and has been a leader in the development of standards for precollege science education, publishing the *National Science Education Standards* in 1995. NRC's Center for Science, Mathematics, and Engineering Education is concerned with curriculum development and review; educational policy; research, assessment, and evaluation; K–12 policy and practice; and postsecondary policy and practice. The National Science Education Standards project has a comprehensive outreach strategy to support national, state, and local implementation of the Standards through leadership and resource development, partnerships and networks, and targeted symposia and workshops. The National Science Resources Center, a joint program of the National Academy of Sciences and the Smithsonian Institution, is concerned with reforming science education and producing resources for teaching science. Project RISE (Regional Initiatives in Science Education) provides scientists and engineers with information and resources to assist them in contributing effectively to K–12 science education partnerships.

National Science Education Leadership Association, P.O. Box 5556, Arlington, VA 22205; (703) 524-8646.

A 1,200-member association of chairpersons, department heads, science supervisors, coordinators, and other leaders in science education reform. The organization's mission is to improve science education through leadership development. Sponsors miniconferences and leadership institutes. Publishes *Science Leadership Trend Notes, NSELA Handbook,* and the *Science Educator* (journal).

National Science Foundation, Directorate for Education and Human Resources, 4201 Wilson Blvd., Arlington, VA 22230; (703) 306-1600.

The Directorate for Education and Human Resources of the National Science Foundation, an independent federal agency, is a major force in science education reform. The Division of Elementary, Secondary, and Informal Education is concerned with curriculum development and teacher enhancement in science, mathematics, and engineering. The Division of Human Resources Development is concerned with broadening the participation of people in underrepresented groups in science, mathematics, and engineering. The Division of Undergraduate Education is concerned with teacher preparation. The Office of Systemic Reform manages three large-scale reform projects: the Rural Systemic Initiatives, Statewide Systemic Initiatives, and Urban Systemic Initiatives. The Rural Systemic Initiatives Program supports efforts to make systemic improvements in science, mathematics, and technology education in rural, economically disadvantaged regions. The Statewide Systemic Initiatives Program supports comprehensive, systemic, statewide efforts to change educational systems and improve science, mathematics, and technology education. The Urban Systemic Initiatives Program supports comprehensive, systemic reform efforts in science, mathematics, and technology education in large urban school systems.

National Science Resources Center, Smithsonian Institution, MRC 502, Arts and Industries Bldg., Rm. 1201, Washington, DC 20560; (202) 357-2555.

Organization sponsored jointly by the National Academy of Sciences and the Smithsonian Institution to contribute to the improvement of science education in the nation's schools. Conducts workshops at National Science Teachers Association and other meetings and holds two annual Leadership Institutes to train teams across the country on science education reform issues and methods. Publications include Science and Technology for Children, a series of 24 core curriculum units (grades 1–6) in the physical, life, and earth sciences and design technology; *Resources for Teaching Elementary School Science* and projected companion volumes for middle and high schools; *Science for All Children: A Guide to Improving Elementary Science Education in Your School District;* and a newsletter.

National Science Teachers Association, 1840 Wilson Blvd., Arlington, VA 22201-3000; (703) 243-7100.

Organization committed to improving science education at all levels (pre-K through college), with a membership of 52,000, including science teachers, supervisors, administrators, scientists, and business and industry representatives. Holds one national and three regional conferences per year; certifies science teachers in eight teaching-level and discipline-area categories; has a computer bulletin board, an employment registry, nearly 20 award programs for teachers, and award programs for students; and gives educational tours. Publications include *Science and Children* (a magazine), *NSTA Reports!* (a newspaper), curriculum units, supplementary activities, and other instructional materials and publications.

National Staff Development Council, P.O. Box 240, Oxford, OH 45056; (513) 523-6029.

Organization responsible for providing assistance and support to local school district staff responsible for the administration, supervision, and coordination of professional development programs. Promotes public policy favorable to the development of comprehensive districtwide professional development programs and provides information on new professional development models, theories of adult learning, planning and funding of district-based programs, and relevant research. Publications include *The Developer* (a newsletter) and *Journal of Staff Development.*

Northwest EQUALS, FAMILY SCIENCE, Portland State University, P.O. Box 1491, Portland, OR 97201-1491; (503) 725-3045.

Regional site for the EQUALS and FAMILY MATH programs produced by EQUALS of Berkeley, California, and the developer and national disseminator of FAMILY SCIENCE, a national outreach program designed to teach science by having children (grades K–8) and parents learn and enjoy science together; modeled after FAMILY MATH and EQUALS, FAMILY SCIENCE addresses the underrepresentation of women and ethnic and racial minorities in the sciences by demonstrating the role science plays in daily life, schooling, and future work. Publications include *FAMILY SCIENCE,* a book about implementing the program.

Office of Elementary and Secondary Education, Smithsonian Institution, Arts and Industries Bldg., Rm. 1163, Washington DC 20560; (202) 357-2425.

The Smithsonian Institution's central office for precollege education, drawing on the entire Smithsonian complex of museums, exhibitions, collections, and staff expertise to create a range of materials and programs. Programs include summer seminars for teachers and Smithsonian On-line on the Internet. Publications include supplemental curriculum materials, "Mystery at the Museum" (a video game), *Art to Zoo* (a journal), and a newsletter.

School Science and Mathematics Association, Department of Curriculum and Foundations, Bloomsburg University, 400 E. Second St., Bloomsburg, PA 17815-1301; (717) 389-4915.

Organization for science and mathematics teachers (elementary science through college) emphasizing integration of science and mathematics. Publications include curriculum units emphasizing science-mathematics integration, *Topics for Teachers* (a monograph series), *Classroom Activities* (a monograph series), *School Science and Mathematics* (a journal), and a newsletter.

Sigma Xi, The Scientific Research Society, 99 Alexander Dr., P.O. Box 13975, Research Triangle Park, NC 22709; (800) 243-6534.

Interdisciplinary honor society of more than 90,000 research scientists and engineers affiliated with some 500 local Sigma XI groups. Programs available through local Sigma Xi groups include teacher-scientist partnerships, speakers bureaus, classroom demonstrations, curriculum development with teachers, sponsorship of science fairs, lab visits for students, and scientist mentors for students. Publications from Society headquarters include *Scientists and Science Education* (annual report on the activities of the local groups), brochures to promote scientist-teacher partnerships and scientist involvement in reform efforts, and names and addresses of the officers of local Sigma Xi groups. Publications and other materials from local groups include curriculum guidelines and units, audiovisual and computer-based materials, and lab equipment and supplies for loan or as a gift.

Society for Advancement of Chicanos and Native Americans in Science, Applied Sciences, Trailer #5, University of California at Santa Cruz, Santa Cruz, CA 95064; (408) 459-4272.

Society of 600 professionals in science and education striving to increase the participation of Latinos and Native Americans in science. Programs include teacher workshops at annual meeting. Publications include a newsletter, with a section on K–12 programs.

TERC, 2067 Massachusetts Ave., Cambridge, MA 02140; (617) 547-0430; e-mail: communications@terc.edu.

Nonprofit education research and development organization focused on science and mathematics learning and teaching. Programs include The Hub, an electronic source of materials and information. Publications and electronic materials include National Geographic Kids Network, developed with the National Geographic Society; LabNet, an electronic community of elementary and secondary teachers that fosters science and mathematics teaching; Tabletop Junior, software for visualization in data collection and analysis; *Hands On!* (periodical on science, math, and technology education); and publications on telecommunications.

Triangle Coalition for Science and Technology Education, 5112 Berwyn Rd., College Park, MD 20740-4129; (301) 220-0870.

Coalition with representation from more than 100 member organizations, including business, industry, labor, scientific and engineering societies, education associations, and government agencies. Works to link national science education reform efforts with local schools and school districts. Organization promotes collaborations and partnerships between teachers and volunteer scientists through several hundred action groups and alliances. Publications include *Guide for Building an Alliance* and *Guide for Planning a Volunteer Program,* both of which address science, mathematics, and technology education; numerous reports on reform efforts, state and federal programs, and other issues in science education; and a newsletter.

U.S. Department of Education, Office of Educational Research and Improvement, 555 New Jersey Ave., N.W., Washington, DC 20208; (202) 219-2050.

An office of the U.S. Department of Education that supports research and disseminates information. This office sponsors 10 Eisenhower Regional Mathematics and Science Education Consortia, which provide information, technical assistance, and training to states, schools, and teachers to help improve mathematics and science programs and adapt and use exemplary instructional materials, teaching methods, curricula, and assessment tools. Located in Andover, Massachusetts; Aurora, Colorado; Austin, Texas; Charleston, West Virginia; Honolulu, Hawaii; Montpelier, Vermont; Oak Brook, Illinois; Philadelphia, Pennsylvania; Portland, Oregon; and Tallahassee, Florida. Also sponsors the National Assessment of Education Progress, which measures educational achievement of students in grades 4, 8, and 12, and, for science, uses a hands-on task and portfolio. Other programs include the National Diffusion Network, a system for disseminating more than 70 programs, products, and processes in mathematics, science, and technology education, and 10 Regional Educational Laboratories that do applied research and development in the areas of educational programs, materials, and professional development.

U.S. Department of Education, Office of Elementary and Secondary Education, 400 Maryland Ave., S.W., Washington, DC 20208; (202) 401-0113.

An office of the U.S. Department of Education supporting elementary and secondary education through programs for compensatory education, school improvement, and special student populations; the Eisenhower Mathematics and Science Education State Formula Grants Program; and the Christa McAuliffe Fellowship Program for outstanding teachers.

U.S. Department of Education, Office of Elementary and Secondary Education, School Effectiveness Division, 600 Independence Ave., S.W., Portals 4500, Washington, DC 20202-6140; (202) 260-2666.

Division in the Office of Elementary and Secondary Education that operates the Eisenhower Professional Development State Grants Program, which supports teacher enhancement programs via state educational agencies. Involved in both in-service and pre-service training.

U.S. Department of the Interior, National Park Service, P.O. Box 37127, Suite 560, Washington, DC 20013-7127; (202) 523-5270.

The National Park Service's Parks as Classrooms Program arranges workshops for teachers at more than 270 sites of the National Park Service to encourage building curricula around National Park resources; many sites have workshops focused at least in part on science.

Appendix B

Exemplary Elementary Science Curriculum Materials

The following curriculum materials meet the criteria outlined in Chapter 5. Materials such as these can create a solid framework around which to build an exemplary elementary science program.

Full Option Science System (FOSS). FOSS Program, Lawrence Hall of Science, University of California, Berkeley, CA 94720. Phone: (510) 642-8941; fax: (510) 642-1055. Distributed by Encyclopaedia Britannica Educational Corporation, 310 South Michigan Ave., Chicago, IL 60604. Phone: (800) 554-9862.

The FOSS program is designed to engage students in actively constructing scientific concepts through multisensory, hands-on laboratory activities. The K–6 curriculum comprises 27 modules: five kindergarten modules organized under topics in the life and physical sciences; six modules for grades 1 and 2 in the areas of life, physical, and earth sciences; and 16 modules for grades 3 to 6 in the life, physical, and earth sciences, as well as in scientific reasoning and technology. Students in grades 1 and 2 explore three modules per year, while students in grades 3 to 6 use four modules per year. A multimedia component is available; it is marketed as the Britannica Science System. Development of the FOSS program was funded by the National Science Foundation.

Improving Urban Elementary Science (Insights). Education Development Center, Inc., 55 Chapel St., Newton, MA 02160. Phone: (617) 969-7100 or (800) 225-4276; fax: (617) 965-6325. Distributed by Kendall Hunt Publishing Company, 4050 Westmark Drive, P.O. Box 1840, Dubuque, IA 52004-1840. Phone: (800) 542-6657.

Insights is a curriculum program made up of 17 modules for grades K through 6, each requiring six to eight weeks to complete. The modules help develop students' understanding of science and encourage problem-solving skills. Topics reflect a balance of life, physical, and earth sciences and can integrate science with other areas of the curriculum, especially language arts and mathematics. The activities in this program support cultural, racial, and linguistic diversity. Funding was provided by the National Science Foundation.

Science and Technology for Children (STC). National Science Resources Center, Arts and Industries Building, Room 1201, Smithsonian Institution, Washington, DC 20560. Phone: (202) 357-2555; fax: (202) 786-2028. Distributed by Carolina Biological Supply Company, 2700 York Rd., Burlington, NC 27215. Phone: (800) 227-1150.

The STC program consists of a series of 24 inquiry-centered curriculum modules for grades 1 through 6, with 4 units at each grade level. The modules cover life, earth, and physical sciences and design technology. The technological applications of science and the interactions among science, technology, and society are addressed throughout the program. The modules are designed to involve children in hands-on, inquiry-based investigations of scientific phenomena. Development of scientific reasoning skills is emphasized. Major support for the STC program has been provided by the National Science Foundation, the John D. and Catherine T. MacArthur Foundation, the U.S. Department of Defense, the Dow Chemical Company Foundation, and the U.S. Department of Education. Other contributors include E. I. du Pont de Nemours & Company, the Amoco Foundation, Inc., and the Hewlett-Packard Company.

Index

Credits

Page 3: Eric Long, Smithsonian Institution/courtesy of National Science Resources Center, Washington, D.C.

Page 13: Illustrations by Max-Karl Winkler

Page 15: Eric Long, Smithsonian Institution/courtesy of National Science Resources Center, Washington, D.C.

Page 18: Eric Long, Smithsonian Institution/courtesy of National Science Resources Center, Washington, D.C.

Page 27: Rick Vargas, Smithsonian Institution/courtesy of National Science Resources Center, Washington, D.C.

Page 44: Eric Long, Smithsonian Institution/courtesy of National Science Resources Center, Washington, D.C.

Page 47: Reproduced with permission from National Science Resources Center, Washington, D.C.

Page 65: Matt Smith/courtesy of National Science Resources Center, Washington, D.C.

Page 80: Rick Vargas, Smithsonian Institution/courtesy of National Science Resources Center, Washington, D.C.

Page 92: Matt Smith/courtesy of National Science Resources Center, Washington, D.C.

Page 102: Rick Vargas, Smithsonian Institution/courtesy of National Science Resources Center, Washington, D.C.

Pages 104–105: Student work by Brandon Weiss and Luke Bostian/courtesy of National Science Resources Center, Washington, D.C.

Page 106–107: Reproduced with permission from *Reading the Environment*, in Insights: An Elementary Hands-on Science Curriculum. Published by Education Development Center, Inc., Newton, MA 02160.

Page 111: Student work by Faith Washington, Daniel Hall, and Lunden Letofsky/courtesy of National Science Resources Center, Washington, D.C.

Page 112: Student work by Shaughn Bischoff, Alex Jaeger, Jenny Minnard, Margaret Pace, Emilee Schultz, and Julie Wilke

Page 114: Reproduced with permission from *Balancing and Weighing,* in the Science and Technology for Children program, National Science Resources Center, Washington, D.C.

Page 115: Reproduced with permission from *Water,* in the Full Option Science System curriculum program. FOSS was developed at the Lawrence Hall of Science, University of California at Berkeley, and is distributed by Encyclopaedia Britannica Educational Corporation (EBEC), 310 South Michigan Ave., Chicago, IL 60604.

Page 116: Reproduced with permission from *Reading the Environment,* in Insights: An Elementary Hands-on Science Curriculum. Published by Education Development Center, Inc., Newton, MA 02160.

Page 125: Matt Smith/courtesy of National Science Resources Center, Washington, D.C.

Page 128: Mark Davis/courtesy of National Science Resources Center, Washington, D.C.

National Science Resources Center
Advisory Board

225

National Science Resources Center

The National Science Resources Center (NSRC) is operated by the Smithsonian Institution and the National Academy of Sciences to improve the teaching of science in the nation's schools. The NSRC collects and disseminates information about exemplary teaching resources, develops and disseminates curriculum materials, and sponsors outreach activities, specifically in the areas of leadership development and technical assistance, to help school districts develop and sustain hands-on, inquiry-centered science programs. The NSRC is located in the Arts and Industries Building of the Smithsonian Institution and in the Capital Gallery Building in Washington, D.C.

National Academy of Sciences

The National Academy of Sciences is a private, nonprofit, self-perpetuating society of distinguished scholars engaged in scientific and engineering research, dedicated to the furtherance of science and technology and to their use for the general welfare. Upon the authority of the charter granted to it by the Congress in 1863, the Academy has a mandate that requires it to advise the federal government on scientific and technical matters. Dr. Bruce M. Alberts is president of the National Academy of Sciences.

National Research Council

The National Research Council was organized by the National Academy of Sciences in 1916 to associate the broad community of science and technology with the Academy's purposes of furthering knowledge and advising the federal government. Functioning in accordance with general policies determined by the Academy, the Council has become the principal operating agency of both the National Academy of Sciences and the National Academy of Engineering in providing services to the government, the public, and the scientific and engineering communities. The Council is administered jointly by both Academies and the Institute of Medicine. Dr. Bruce M. Alberts and Dr. William A. Wulf are chairman and interim vice chairman, respectively, of the National Research Council.

Smithsonian Institution

The Smithsonian Institution was created by an act of Congress in 1846 in accordance with the will of the Englishman James Smithson, who in 1826 bequeathed his property to the United States of America "to found at Washington, under the name of the Smithsonian Institution, an establishment for the increase and diffusion of knowledge among men." The Smithsonian has since evolved into an institution devoted to public education, research, and national service in the arts, sciences, and history. This independent federal establishment is the world's largest museum complex and is responsible for public and scholarly activities, exhibitions, and research projects nationwide and overseas.